the secret lives of
LITTERBUGS

the secret lives of

LITTERBUGS

and other (true) stories

m.a.c. farrant

KEY PORTER BOOKS

Library and Archives Canada Cataloguing in Publication

Farrant, M. A. C. (Marion Alice Coburn), 1947-
    The secret lives of litterbugs / M.A.C. Farrant.

ISBN 978-1-55470-159-9

    1. Farrant, M. A. C. (Marion Alice Coburn), 1947-. 2. Authors, Canadian
(English)—20th century—Biography. I. Title.

PS8561.A76Z475 2009   C813'.54   C2008-906742-8

ONTARIO ARTS COUNCIL
CONSEIL DES ARTS DE L'ONTARIO

The publisher gratefully acknowledges the support of the Canada Council for the Arts
and the Ontario Arts Council for its publishing program. We acknowledge the support of
the Government of Ontario through the Ontario Media Development Corporation's Ontario Book Initiative.

We acknowledge the financial support of the Government of Canada through the Book
Publishing Industry Development Program (BPIDP) for our publishing activities.

Key Porter Books Limited
Six Adelaide Street East, Tenth Floor
Toronto, Ontario
Canada M5C 1H6

www.keyporter.com

Text design: Marijke Friesen
Electronic formatting: Alison Carr

Printed and bound in Canada

09 10 11 12 13 5 4 3 2 1

For Leslie Willis & Jo-Anne Dobell
Esteemed sisters-in-law

And for Rickey James Farrant
In loving memory

CONTENTS

part 1
SOONER

THE SECRET LIVES OF LITTERBUGS

"People (in the 50s & 60s) painted with lead, insulated with asbestos, smoked after coition, and had one for the road after leaving a party."

Edward Hoagland
Harpers Magazine, August 2003

WE WERE DRIVING ALONG Highway 99 in Oregon State during the summer of 1961 when we first saw a giant cartoon bug painted on a billboard. Alongside the picture were the words: *Don't Be a Litterbug! Pick Up Your Garbage!*

We laughed when we saw the sign. "Would you look at *that?*"

We were on vacation and that sign was another thing to roar past on the way to the next motel, the one with the adjoining Frontier restaurant specializing in steaks the size of saddles.

The litterbug had a black eye patch, green wings, a black and yellow striped body like a bee, and smoked a cigarette. There was a mound of garbage at the litterbug's feet.

A bug was telling us to clean up our garbage. We laughed our heads off; the idea was absurd: there was no family cleaner than ours.

Ernie, my uncle, continually stated the obvious. "What are we, bums?" he'd snort, incredulous, if he found empty pop bottles or gum wrappers inside the car. Riding around in a car filled with garbage was a disgusting thing to do, he said, like riding in the back of a garbage truck and being covered with stinking muck. That's what he called it—stinking muck.

If I was remiss and left a potato chip bag on the car seat, Ernie would notice right away. Even while driving. Elsie, his wife and my aunt—the one who was raising me—said he had eyes in the back of his head. "You can't get away with nothing with Ernie. So do as you're told and throw that bag out the bloody window."

Unlike the Litterbug, there was no mound of garbage at Ernie's feet.

Ernie's vigilance was helped along by the fact that he was the janitor at the Victoria Public Library. He seemed always on duty, prowling the house and yard, keys dangling from the ring attached to his belt. If things weren't spic and span, watch out! "Germs," he'd say, ominously, "hide *everywhere.*"

Elsie was the same. She sprayed Raid around the house like air freshener.

You'd have thought my aunt and uncle's zealousness would have translated to the outside world. It didn't. The outside world was called "out there" and, aside from sunsets and days at the beach, it was a boring place, useful for driving over—and for dumping your garbage.

My father, Billy, was Elsie's brother and he thought the

same way. He worked on the docks in Vancouver and visited us every other weekend. With Billy everything had to be "squared away." He said he'd learned this important thing at sea. He also said, "When you live in a stinking mess you can't see what's what." He told me to remember this; it was one of "Life's Truths."

But it was Ernie who was our standard-bearer as far as travelling garbage went. He made a big production of tossing his cigarette package out the car window. The package went as soon as the last cigarette was hanging off his lip. But first he'd extract the silver foil the cigarettes were wrapped in, fold the two pieces carefully, and then put them into his wallet next to the thick wad of dollar bills. He did this while driving, lifting his bum off the seat in a delicate maneuver to get at the wallet, and then lifting it again to return it there.

Why Ernie saved cigarette foil was a mystery. "Wouldn't you like to know?" he'd smirk, giving me the idea that janitors were people with secret lives. Because I didn't know *exactly* what that secret life might be, I made one up. It happened, I decided, after supper each night when, cranky as usual, he'd lock himself in his workshop off the carport. Inside, I imagined him sitting on the stool beside his prized possession, a huge new table saw, and "working away at his hobby"— fashioning tiny airplanes out of cigarette foil. A hobby, I knew, was something grown men were supposed to have. A hobby kept a man busy so he wouldn't be bothering his wife for sex. Elsie had told me this. I was fourteen that summer and kept close watch on my aunt and uncle's marriage for clues about what lay ahead for me. And a man needing a hobby was a crucial thing to know about married life.

"Management" was what Elsie called marriage: "The State of Holy Management." She'd explained this to me many times. "Men don't know which end is up," she'd say.

"They're clueless. But still, you've got to be kind. You don't want them going around thinking they've got no equipment. That's a recipe for trouble!"

"Eeee uuuu!" my friends squealed when I told them this. "Ballzzzzz!"

LATER THAT SUMMER we were driving up-Island on a family outing. As usual, we weren't paying attention to the scenery. We were looking for the next sign—not the one with the Litterbug but the one that promised a glass castle constructed entirely of embalming fluid bottles. It was somewhere past Duncan. That's where we were headed, a sweaty two-hour drive from Cordova Bay, the thinly populated beach area outside of Victoria where we lived.

There were six of us jammed inside the Zephyr: Elsie; Ernie; Billy; my other aunt, Maudie, a widow; Grandma, who lived with Maudie; and me.

Ernie was driving. He always drove because Billy liked to navigate, liked to estimate the times of arrivals and departures, the ETAs and ETDs, liked to arrive at a destination without any hitches. He'd studied navigation at sea and could, if required, navigate by the stars.

"Never set your sights by the moon," he told me often, another one of "Life's Truths."

Elsie was squished between Ernie and Billy in the front seat. "Shoot, we're stuck together like pigs," she laughed, pulling a damp arm away from Ernie's shoulder. Her flesh was as white as lard.

In the back seat Grandma hummed nursery rhymes, tapping time with her feet which were perched on the hump between the seats. Maudie sat on one side of Grandma; I sat on the other.

We were travelling along, and I remember feeling mildly content. Usually the prospect of a drive with my strangely configured family—Nancy, my mother, had been on "a long trip" for nine years by then—brought a flat-out refusal. But not this day. I was as eager to visit the Glass Castle as everyone else. We'd heard there was a glass elephant's head attached to the outside wall, and a glass Coke bottle twenty feet high. There was even a gift shop.

"What's embalming fluid?" I hollered above the wind.

"It's used to make dead people look alive," Elsie said, twisting towards me. "For the funeral. They used it on Fred. Remember Fred, Ernie? He never looked so good. His skin was like wax."

Ernie grunted.

"I can't see it," Billy said. "Using embalming fluid bottles to make a castle. It doesn't make sense. There aren't enough dead people in these parts. They probably used pop bottles."

Grandma, meanwhile, sat clacking her false teeth. It was a pleasant sound, like a horse sauntering down a tree-lined street on a summer's day. A horse named Daisy wearing a straw hat. ·

After a while she hummed "Three Blind Mice."

Perhaps our casual habit of throwing garbage out the car window gave her the idea for what she did next. In one fluid movement she pulled the teeth from her mouth, reached across me, and flung them out the window. She did this as naturally as if she was getting rid of an empty chip bag. Vaguely, I wondered if Ernie would be pleased.

According to the sign we'd just passed, the teeth landed about ten miles south of the Glass Castle.

"Grandma's thrown her teeth out the window!" I screamed, delighted. "Back there by the sign!"

Ernie screeched to a halt by the side of the road. A cloud of dust plunged into the car.

Elsie hung over the car seat and shrieked, "What did you do that for?"

Grandma's eyes darted about bright and mad. Then she shrugged. Then she sucked on her cheeks and her whole face collapsed.

Billy pushed his baseball cap back on his head and sighed. He pulled the pencil from behind his ear. Here was a hitch: his ETA would need revising.

"Oh, Ma," Maudie said, a wretched look on her face.

"Oh, Ma, nothing," Elsie hissed. "I knew something like this would happen. Something always happens. Didn't I say those very words this morning, Ernie? Didn't I say, 'Just once I'd like to go someplace and have nothing happen'?"

"She should be in a Home," Ernie said quietly, but everyone heard.

"Don't talk stupid," Elsie said. "We should put you in a Home. You and the bloody TV set."

We were stopped by a farm field. Cars sped by, rocking the Zephyr.

I'd seen Grandma's teeth lots of times when I'd stayed over at Maudie's house—at night, on her bedside table. They lay at the bottom of a glass of water, top and bottom joined at the back like a set of castanets.

"Ernie!" Elsie suddenly shouted. "Turn the car around! We've got to find those teeth!"

Turning the car around was something Ernie was already doing. He shot Elsie a murderous look and asked her if she'd finally gone off her rocker.

Elsie gasped. "Of all the bloody—!"

I yelled, "Hurry up! The teeth might get stolen!" I don't know why I said this. I felt urgent, caught up in the drama.

Elsie told me to pipe down. Everything, she said, was getting on her nerves.

Ernie told us both to quit squawking. Sweat was running down his face.

"Quit yer damn squawking," is what he said.

Right then and there I decided I was never getting married. Elsie and Ernie were not a good advertisement for the married life. Marriage was a bad movie staring Bette Davis, who poisons her husband and then watches him die. They're on the porch of their plantation house. "Not feeling well, darling?" Bette asks smoothly, eyes wide with fake innocence. Then stares placidly at the slaves toiling in the cotton fields while her husband writhes at her feet.

"SLOW DOWN. There's the sign!" Billy yelled. He'd been watching the road like a lookout.

It was a homemade sign, white lettering on plywood: Glass Castle—10 Miles. When the car stopped I was the first one out. We were parked beside a steep ditch. Beyond the ditch, farm land stretched to a line of trees in the distance. The silence felt eerie.

"Sheesh!" Ernie said, hauling himself out of the car and looking around. "We're in the middle of nowhere."

Elsie got busy and emptied the car ashtray, heaping cigarette butts and ashes onto the roadside like an offering.

"Now what?" Ernie said, wiping his glasses with a hankie and casting an approving glance at his wife stooped over the road.

Everyone looked to Billy, the navigator, not Ernie, for instructions. Ernie's expertise was travelling garbage. But making decisions in a catastrophe? That was Billy's department.

Billy put one foot on the car bumper, shielded his eyes

from the sun, and stared up and down the road. Waiting for what he had to say, we gazed about helplessly—at the dry fields, the bleached sky with its few wispy clouds.

Finally he turned to us. "We'll have to find those teeth. You can head up there," he told Elsie and Ernie, pointing north. "Have a look in the grass by the side of the road." To me he said, "You and Maudie look the other way. I'll take the ditch by the sign." This was a sacrifice, we knew, because there was no way the rest of us could tackle the ditch: Elsie, Maudie and me in dresses, Ernie because he was fat and broke out in a sweat when he climbed a flight of stairs.

Ernie grumbled. "Ma could at least look for her own teeth."

"That's the most ridiculous thing I've ever heard," Elsie snapped.

Which was true: Ernie was being ridiculous. Grandma was eighty-seven years old and gaga. Maudie said she had to watch her like a hawk. I often forgot she was Elsie's, Maudie's, and Billy's mother. She was just my daft old Grandma. You dressed her up and put her in the car.

I watched Elsie start off in a huff. From head to foot she was peeved. Every time a car went by her dress flared up to her knees and she slapped at it angrily. Because of the heat, she'd rolled her stockings to her ankles. She stumbled along in high heels.

Maudie and I headed the other way. It was hot searching the roadside. There was the pounding sun, the dust and, between passing cars, that heavy silence. After we'd walked a quarter of a mile Billy waved at us to return.

When we got back to the car he was sitting sideways in the passenger seat with his shoes and socks off picking gravel from between his toes. Elsie and Ernie were back and Elsie was pouring tea from the picnic thermos into six green plastic cups. She'd lined up the cups on the hood of the car like a special hood ornament. Inside the car, the teeth sat on the dashboard. Billy had found them at the side of the ditch, not far from the Glass Castle sign. There were chips out of several teeth, but the set was still joined. Maudie said finding the teeth was a miracle. Ernie said he'd walked up the road for nothing and Elsie told him to shut up or she'd throw something at him.

Then Maudie handed round the tin of cookies.

Grandma put a cookie to her mouth and stopped. "Where's my teeth?"

"You threw them out the window," Elsie said.

"I did not. You're always fibbing."

"Oh, forget it," Elsie said. "What's the point?" She got the teeth from the car and rinsed them with tea. "Here," she said, giving them to Grandma. "Put them in."

Grandma took the teeth. I heard the sucking sound as she put them back in her mouth.

Later that day we discovered that Grandma had left her purse behind at the Glass Castle sign though nobody worried about this. The purse was old, and stuffed with folded newspaper, something Grandma insisted on doing each time she left the house. We found it on the way home. Ernie shook it out right away. "Nuff's nuff," he said.

We watched the newspaper blow across the nearby field.

"Looks like big confetti," said Elsie.

"Kinda beautiful," Maudie sighed.

And then we drove away.

PORK CHOPS

IT WAS NO SECRET to me as a young teenager that Elsie's main job as a wife was to keep Ernie busy around the house and yard, keep him diverted so he wouldn't be prone to getting the sex-crazed eyes that all wives feared. Sex-crazed eyes, I knew by now, could happen in a flash if a woman wasn't vigilant. "Keep a man well-fed and worn out," Elsie often said. "Then your life will be your own."

Having a life of your own was hard to reconcile with the pamphlet my friend Valerie and I found in her mother's drawer. We read it as our future and were appalled. "A woman's body belongs to her husband, so it's important to keep it clean and well-groomed." There was a drawing of a fully-clothed woman lying like a corpse on top of a double bed. Her eyes were closed. She wasn't smiling. She was waiting—dutifully? resignedly?—for her sex-crazed husband to pounce on her.

"Oh, barf!" we screamed.

Still, if anyone could avoid that poor woman's fate it was

Elsie. I'd often watch her going about the important work of keeping the beast at bay. But who could figure harmless old Ernie as a beast? Was he really prone to "urges"? And, like all men, did these "urges" cause him to lose his mind?

Ernie wore thick, black-framed glasses, and I became curious as to what lay behind them. It was difficult to get a good look at his eyes because of the glasses but I wanted to get a reading, see if his eyes were even remotely sex-crazed, though I wasn't sure what sex-crazed eyes look like. Wild? Mean? Insane? Bugged out like the Little Moron's?

I found an opportunity to make an observation one afternoon while he was watching *The Three Stooges*. Joining him for the show, I dropped my bag of chips at his feet so I could get a close look at his eyes while picking it up. Nose to nose I peered through his smudged glasses.

"Whatcha doin?"

"Nothing."

"Well, quit it. You're giving me the creeps."

Ernie's eyes were disappointing. They were dull brown in colour, and about as crazed looking as a puppy's. But then maybe Ernie was simply exhausted, the result of Elsie's successful campaign. He was too pooped to do anything but drag on his cigarette, stare at the TV.

I wondered further. What about sex-crazed behaviour? What did *that* look like? Constant drooling? Chasing Elsie around the house with his tongue hanging out when I was at school? Acting like an ape?

As far as I knew Ernie did none of these things. But maybe there were other less obvious signs that I didn't know about. Watching my squat, bald uncle in his grey janitor's clothes going about his regular life—taking out the garbage, washing the outside windows, sucking on a piece of *Cadbury's Pure Milk Chocolate*—I couldn't imagine what these other signs might be. True, he often licked his full, purplish lips. But this wasn't drooling. This was because he had something stuck to them—pieces of chocolate, tobacco, cookie crumbs, cat hair, peas, and, once, a small dust bunny.

Elsie had a war going against Ernie and the TV set. She must have decided that too much TV meant the sex fiend that lived inside him was resting up, gaining enough energy to pounce on her when she least expected it. She must have been constantly looking over her shoulder while she worked at the sewing machine, or scrubbed the kitchen floor on her hands and knees, or planted Naughty Mariettas in the border alongside the house. This would explain why she was frequently on edge: she was on the lookout in case Ernie's beast reared its ugly...eeee uuuu! I always stopped there.

This is how she operated. Ernie would be plunked down with his chocolate bar in front of the TV set before supper, grinning away at the show, oblivious to everything except *The Adventures of Mighty Mouse*, when Elsie would suddenly bawl, "Ernie! The grass needs cutting!" "The garbage!" "What about the drain pipes?" "There's an ants' nest in the basement!" "The sink's plugged!"

We never knew for sure when she'd go off, but you could pretty well count on it happening any time Ernie was still— drinking tea, watching cartoons, hiding out in his workshop. Her kamikaze screaming raised neck hairs and stopped hearts. Before the TV Ernie would jolt as if he'd been smacked, and then shuddering, resettle in his chair, light up another cigarette, take a long, weary drag, blow smoke rings, pick the stray bits of tobacco from his lips, and then, with a heavy sigh, try to re-enter Mighty Mouse's universe. None of this was of any use.

"Well?" Elsie would bellow from the doorway.

"Well what?" he'd answer hopelessly.

"I can't make supper with a bloody sink that's plugged."

And then he'd heave himself from his chair, and head out the front door.

"Where are you going?"

"To get my tool box," he'd growl, barely audible. "Or do you think I can fix the sink with my bloody teeth?"

WEIRDLY, Elsie and Ernie's last name was Sexton. It was right there in the phone book: E. Sexton. Kids and panting men were always calling us up. "Got any sex for sale?" "Is this the *Sex* house?" We became adept at slamming down the receiver whenever we heard pipsqueak giggles or heavy breathing on the other end of the line. Heavy breathing—another clue?

I thought that having sex in their name was a riot because, as far as I knew, Elsie managed Ernie so well that they never did it. He was too exhausted—up at 5 every morning to get to the library by 6; all those household chores he had to complete, day in day out. My bedroom was next to theirs and all I ever heard was snoring, and the odd yelp from Ernie.

"Keep stubbing my toe," he'd say, when I'd ask about the yelp.

But more than sex-crazed men, and sex, in particular—which terrified me, both the badly understood mechanics of it, and the disastrous life-ruining result if you got knocked up—I yearned to know first-hand about love and romance. Surely this was something that existed—like a placid meadow hidden within a forest that you'd unexpectedly come upon and be delighted by. Even though I didn't see romantic evidence between the men and women in my family—the only kisses were demure pecks at Christmas or birthdays, no one held hands, no one uttered the word "love"—I was desperate for proof.

Elsie's usual comment on the subject of romantic love was to snort. "Hah! Only in the movies. Real love's nothing to write home about. It's a two-faced beast. Sweet before the wedding to lure you in. Cranky for the next forty years."

Elsie's views were supported in chorus by her married daughter Doreen; by her other married daughter Shirley who was living in California and presumably spreading the word down there; by Grandma before she'd gone gaga; and by her sister, Maudie.

I HAD THE OPPORTUNITY to ask questions about love one stormy Saturday afternoon in November when Doreen, Grandma, and Maudie were visiting. We were having tea in the kitchen when Elsie started in on her favourite topic.

"Men. You're damned if you do, and damned if you don't," she declared. "There's no pleasing them. I've had it about up to here." She sliced her neck viciously with her hand.

What had ticked her off—again—was Ernie. He'd gone off pork chops. "You try to give them what they like, and they turn on you," she said.

"How?" I asked, the eager disciple.

"They make a sour face and act hurt," she answered, suddenly changing gears, telling the story like a joke. We were all ears. "How was I supposed to know he'd gone off bloody pork chops? Pork chops have always been his favourite supper. But do you think he'd say something? Do you think we'd have a conversation about it? Oh, no, not him. Keeps his trap shut. I'm supposed to be a mind reader. That's me, Madam Elsie, the mind reader with a crystal ball."

Everyone laughed except Grandma. She was playing solitaire at the end of the table and looked up when she heard the rest of us laugh. "Ha, ha, ha," she said, the words keeping time with the nursery rhyme she'd been humming, "Pease Porridge Hot."

"Two bloody pork chops!" Elsie continued. "Last night at the supper table. Fried just the way he likes 'em. With the fat all burnt. There he was, poking and picking at 'em like they'd gone bad. Putting his nose to the plate and sniffing. Like this."

She demonstrated for us, bending over the table and sniffing the tabletop. Doreen let out a scream.

I'd been at the pork chop supper but didn't remember the sniffing part. What I did remember, though, was (unspoken) Rule Number One: Anything for a laugh; anything for a good story.

"He acted like I was trying to poison him," Elsie continued. "'What's the matter with you?' I said. And he looked at me like he'd just pulled his head out of a garbage can. His face all pinched and snooty." Here Elsie scrunched up her face in another imitation and nodded her head, side to side, while everyone laughed some more.

"What happened next?" I asked.

"I'm getting to it," she said. "Don't rush me." (Rule Number Two: Take your time). "He just looked at me like I was a blank wall, and said, 'I'm sick of pork chops.' Just like that. 'You're sick of pork chops? Well, thanks for telling me,' I said. 'You could have let me know.'" Here Elsie changed her tone, became thin-lipped, severe. "Now he won't talk to me. Gone out to his bloody shop. He can move the cot out there for all I care. Go live in his shop. Cook his own bloody meals. I've been getting the silent treatment since last night."

Doreen, married for six years by now and Elsie's main confidante, said resignedly, "Makes you mad when they do that."

Elsie stubbed out her cigarette and took up the teapot for pouring. "Damn right it makes you mad. For two cents I'd chuck him in the ocean. I'd chuck *all* men in the ocean. What's the good of 'em?"

I could swear the house shook after this declaration, but it may have been the storm. It continued unabated outside the kitchen window with lashing rain, screaming gulls. Ernie had built our small house; it was perched rather dramatically on the cliffside overlooking Cordova Bay. This was fine in summer when the view was spectacular and the weather balmy, but because the house was so exposed it bore the brunt of winter storms; the wind blew mercilessly through the cracks around the windows in the sea-facing front room. Elsie combated this problem by hanging grey wool blankets across the doorless opening to this room, the result being that most of the house's natural light was shut out as well.

That afternoon all the lights were on in the house and the electric heat was cranked up past eighty though the kitchen thermometer said sixty-eight.

Grandma, meanwhile, had started a whispery chant: "Ha, ha, ha." She was standing now and drawing circles on the steamed up kitchen window. "Ha, ha, ha," got her halfway down a circle, then another "Ha, ha, ha," got her to the top.

Elsie ignored Grandma's background music and carried on talking. "Butter would melt in his mouth when I've given him pork chops before. Why the change all of a sudden?" She lit another cigarette. We watched the smoke drift across the cookie plate.

"It's different when you're in love, isn't it?" I said to the table.

Three faces looked at me with frank astonishment.

"What do you mean?" Elsie asked, suspicious.

"Love. When you're in love. It's different than with pork

chops, isn't it? It's all...I don't know...good."

Doreen immediately went dreamy.

Elsie said, "Hah!" But she was thinking it over. "The beginning part's okay," she conceded. "I'll give you that. The flowers and nice manners. They way they fall over you like cocker spaniels. But it don't last. It never does. The bloom is soon off the rose."

Maudie, who never said much about men, except to nod helplessly when the subject came up, was now smiling inwardly. "I had a lovely wedding," she said at length. "I made the dress myself. I even sewed pearls on the bodice." She turned to Elsie and laughed. "Remember the bagpipes? I walked down the aisle to bagpipes!"

Doreen's face lit up. "We had a dance band at my wedding. You wore a little yellow dress," she said, turning to me happily. "And little white shoes. Remember that, Marion? You were only eight years old."

Elsie let out an impatient sigh. "And it all ends up with being sick of bloody pork chops."

I asked, "What was your wedding like? To Ernie. Was there music? What did you wear?"

"There was no music," Elsie said briskly. "I wore a blue suit with a matching pillbox hat. Your father walked me down the aisle because Pa was drunk. What more do you want to know?"

"Did you go on a honeymoon?"

"We went to Seattle for the weekend. By boat. I got seasick."

"That must have been fun," Doreen said.

"None of it was fun. You were at Maudie's refusing to live with us after the wedding. I couldn't do a thing with you. You were awful. Said you'd rather die."

"I *was* awful," Doreen grinned. "I didn't like Pop at

first." In the last few years she'd taken to calling Ernie, her step-father, "Pop." Her real father had died of TB when she was fourteen.

"Then what?" I asked. "After the wedding."

"Then nothing. This house. You coming to live with us when you were five. The girls getting married."

She gave me a level look. "What's all this talk about love, anyway? What's going on?"

"Nothing. I was just wondering."

"Well, don't bother. It never pays to get moony over a man. Every minute of every day some stupid girl is being hoodwinked by the promise in a Valentine's Day card."

"Valentine's Day only comes once a year," I said, happy to trip her up.

"Don't be ridiculous," she said. "You know what I mean."

There was a rare lull then around the table. Rain continued pelting the house. The clouds were so low down and dark you couldn't see the ocean. Gusts of wind buckled the windows.

"Look, there's Mr. Magoo," Doreen cried. All of Grandma's circling had cleared the window of steam and we could see out.

Ernie's pet seagull was perched shakily on the clothesline pole near the side of the house; he wobbled in the wind. Ernie fed him bread crusts every day after work. When the seagull saw Ernie it would fly down and patter towards him on thin, pink legs.

I wondered now about Ernie in his workshop, and what he was doing. He had an electric heater in there; he had his chocolate bars, his silver foil. He was probably making airplanes, I decided, though the thought of him flying them while a storm raged outside was sad—the brief ascent, the nosedive onto the cement floor. I wondered briefly about the men in the family. Did they find the women as awful as we apparently found them? Ernie; Doreen's husband, Bob; Maudie's son Kenny; Billy when he was over. They seemed happy enough, watching *Wide World of Sports* together on Sunday afternoons, passing around the bowl of *Cheezies*, filling in the long stretch until the roast at 5.

"Mr. Magoo's hungry," I said. "Ernie hasn't fed him today."

"There's an idea," Elsie said, cheering up. "I'll put Mr. Magoo in a stew. See how his lordship likes that!"

Doreen chortled, but I screamed, "Elsie!"

Maudie bit into a cookie, and then spoke. "When Frank was alive, I rolled his cigarettes for him every night. And put them by his side of the bed so he'd have one when he woke up. One night I didn't make enough and he nudged me in the ribs. 'I'm out of fags,' he said. So I got up at three in the morning and rolled him four more."

"I would have shoved the bloody cigarettes down his throat," Elsie said. "Why you put up with it I'll never know. The way you ran after him. But that's men for you. Think of no one but themselves."

Maudie shrugged, and grinned sheepishly. "Oh well," she said.

Doreen patted her hand. "Uncle Frank was a good provider," she said loudly, as if to a deaf person. "He left you well off, didn't he? You've got his Navy pension. The house all paid for."

"Umm," Maudie said.

Grandma said, "Ha, ha, ha, ha, ha," only louder now, stomping her feet up and down in a stationary march.

"Oh, Ma, put a sock in it," Elsie said.

Grandma stuck out her tongue, and continued stomping.

"Maybe Ernie's sick," Maudie suggested kindly. "Maybe that's why he couldn't eat the pork chops."

"Oh, you don't think so, do you?" Doreen added, worried. She cried easily. Already her eyes were brim-full.

"Sick, my eye!" Elsie boomed. "He ate half an apple pie last night watching TV. And that was before his bedtime snack!"

Clearing away the tea things her mood abruptly softened. "What about Ernie in the workshop?" she said. "He's pouted long enough. And it's cold out there. The shop heater don't always work."

"He'll turn into a Pop-sicle," I said. "Get it?"

No one paid any attention to me. (Rule Number Three: Pick Your Moments). All eyes were on Elsie.

"Want me to bang on the shop door? See if he wants tea?" Doreen asked.

"Can if you like. I'll put the kettle on for a fresh pot. But he better not mention pork chops again. Honestly, I could have spit," Elsie laughed, a sign that their fight was over, and turned towards the sink.

Ten minutes later we watched as Ernie took the offered cup of tea from Elsie. He looked harmless enough standing there in his slippers and old blue cardigan; there was no way I could imagine him being "sex-crazed." Beneath the glare of the kitchen light you couldn't see his eyes through his glasses, couldn't guess what he was thinking. He said nothing to us, which wasn't unusual; he often acted wary before a group of women. Elsie had wedged four chocolate chip cookies around his cup and saucer, two more than his usual share. He took the cup without comment and padded off for the TV set in the den.

Elsie winked at us behind his back.

I was struck by that wink. Maybe she loves him after all, I thought. Maybe that wink is proof.

BAKED SALMON

RIGHT FROM THE START Martin Defolio knew my position on sex. Knew that I was saving myself, not for marriage, but from the disaster of being knocked up. This terrible thing had recently happened to Rhonda Tuttle. One weekend my girlfriends and I were dancing at her pajama party and the next she was crying her eyes out in a home for unwed mothers. We were fifteen and this was 1962. Instantly Rhonda Tuttle's life was over. When she heard the news, Elsie said with relish, "Now maybe you'll understand what's what. You don't want to end up at shit creek without a paddle like Rhonda Tuttle, do you? Her poor mother could just about die."

The thing was, shit creek had its attractions and, notwithstanding the certainty that sex would ruin my life, Martin Defolio was one of them. I'd met him the previous summer in front of Woolworth's department store in Victoria while working part-time as an Ambassadorette, one of three girls hired to promote the city's centennial—1862 to 1962.

He was standing with two other guys, sharing a cigarette. The sun was shining on his stiff, curvy hair; he was tall and skinny and wore a slouchy black and brown-striped sweater over stovepipe pants; he gave me a cynical and weary smile when I stared at him. On top of that Martin Defolio oozed *bad*. My impression was confirmed when Nadine, one of the other Ambassadorettes, who was a Victoria girl, said his brother was in jail.

We were dressed in grey slacks, high heels, red velvet tail coats, and grey top hats. "Buy a Booster Button? Support Victoria's Centennial?" we'd holler at passersby. We looked like hat-check girls in the movies with our trays of buttons slung around our necks, our top hats tilted over one eye. I asked Martin Defolio that day if he wanted one of my buttons. He smiled slightly, licked his narrow lips, then looked at his friends and winked. Finally he tossed a quarter onto my tray and asked for my phone number. I wrote it on the back of his cigarette package.

I lied to Elsie about Martin Defolio's age. Otherwise I wouldn't be allowed to date him.

I said he was sixteen.

I said he was on the honour role at school.

I said he wanted to be an accountant when he grew up, like Mr. Holt next door who was so rich he took his family to Hawaii for two weeks every Christmas.

Elsie liked the idea of my dating a future rich boy. She said, "Well, isn't that nice. We'll have to invite Martin to dinner."

Alarmed, I told her he didn't eat dinner. Only mashed carrots and milkshakes, that he had a problem with his stomach. I didn't want her inspecting him up close.

Elsie called him a poor skinny thing and asked if he maybe ate fish.

I said I didn't think so, that he fed himself with a tube. Elsie said, "Is that a fact?"

After a couple of dates I got to know what Martin Defolio was like. He may have been good-looking and owned a car—a lowered Mercury splattered with orange primer—but he wasn't that smart. He was nineteen and still in Grade 10 at Victoria High School; they kept him for the basketball. And he was incapable of speaking in distinct words. "Wazzawannado?" he'd ask. I soon started replying in a similar fashion—"Idunnowhachoowannado?" But conversation wasn't the point of Martin Defolio; the point was being seen in a car with an older boy from Victoria, with someone who was the exact opposite of the buzz-cut twerps at my Cordova Bay school, a place that qualified as the boonies.

The point was impressing my friends. To them I started calling Martin Mr. Puke. This was because during each "date" while parked at the White Spot Drive-In he'd get drunk on vodka and Orange Crush and throw up out the car window. Chunks of cheeseburger and fries would splash onto the side of his car, the Drive-In parking lot, the rolling pavement of Douglas Street. Sometimes he'd try to get in my pants and *then* throw up. This was not a comment on my performance. There was no performance. There was only barf. We'd be parked up at Mt. Tolmie overlooking the lights of Victoria with all the other fogged-up cars bouncing away nearby, and Martin would get slobbery. His bony hand would start crawling up my leg, an inch at a time, as if this was a war (it was!) and his hand was a creeping soldier with a grenade gripped between his teeth.

"My aunt was right," I'd later shriek to my friends, relating another tale of fighting off the beast. "All a guy wants to do is to haul out his gearshift and ruin your life!"

After taking me home weekend nights—I had an 11 p.m. curfew—Martin drag raced down Yates Street in Victoria. There was a front page story in the *Victoria Daily Times* complaining about this. Martin and his friends, though unnamed, were called "a gang of juvenile delinquents."

"It's not the same guy," I told Elsie after she'd read the story and was looking at me with narrowed eyes. "It's someone else."

I took the newspaper to school. "That's *him*! That's *him!*"

SOON AFTER, Elsie decided it was time to invite Martin to Sunday dinner. I tried to thwart the invitation by citing his "eating problem" but Elsie was determined. She asked him herself on a Friday night when he picked me up for our usual drive and park and puke at the White Spot.

Dinner was to be baked salmon, a dish that nobody in my family liked. But we were having it, Elsie told me pointedly, because I'd given her the idea that fish was the only thing that Martin Defolio could eat. A lot of trouble went into preparing the meal—cookbooks were checked, phone calls made. How many minutes per pound in the oven? Covered or not?

With the salmon we were having mashed potatoes, frozen peas, and turnips and carrots, also mashed. A bowl of lemon wedges sat on the table beside the rectangle of margarine. The best knives and forks and plates were used for the settings, the best paper napkins.

At 4:30 I hung around the kitchen. "How much longer?" Martin was the first boy I'd ever had to supper and I was nervous, not only because there was a good chance my lie about his age and his eating habits would be discovered, but because I didn't like him very much by then and worried that my family would think we were in love.

Elsie said, "What's the rush?"

Doreen, who along with her husband Bob and three-year-old Lyn had dinner with us every Sunday, smirked and nodded towards the den where Martin was watching *Wide World of Sports* and drinking beer with Ernie and Bob. "He's a big hit!" she said.

Elsie agreed, sounding pleased. "It's like old home week in there. And he's such a nice boy. So polite. Not anything like a juvenile delinquent."

All I could do was groan.

We sat down to eat at twenty to six, late because Elsie wasn't sure the fish was cooked. Bowls of food were set out on the table, something that was not usually done; supper was always dished up at the stove.

We were eating at the grey Arborite kitchen table with the chrome legs. The top of it was designed to look like marble. Everyone had a full glass of milk before them.

Martin Defolio and I sat on one side of the table; Doreen, Bob, and Lyn were jammed on the other side; Elsie and Ernie sat at either end. I was expecting someone to say grace, as a joke. This often happened at "formal" meals: "Grace? Grace? Anybody seen Grace?" "She's not here! She moved to Podunk, Saskatchewan!" But this didn't happen.

Then I was afraid someone would look in the window and see Martin and me sitting side-by-side like a married couple, and split a gut, and tell everyone at school and then the whole school would split a gut.

When we had the napkins placed on our laps Bob hollered, "Pass the smashed potatoes," spreading his grin all round like the goofball he was.

Elsie said sternly, "Pass Martin the food first." Everyone did. He sat bewildered with three bowls and the salmon platter in an arc before him while the rest of us stared, watching what he'd take first. He took the peas.

Then Ernie opened up the dinner conversation. "They're calling for snow."

Elsie said happily, "I love snow. One time when I was a kid we skated outdoors." She'd taken off her apron. She wore one of her good dresses, the purple crepe with the fancy stitching on the bodice as befitted a "special occasion." She had on her rhinestone glasses.

"How do you skate in snow?" Ernie asked sarcastically, catching Bob's eye. He ambushed Elsie every now and then when strangers were around and she couldn't be her true self and scream at him to go jump in the lake.

"Never mind," she said briskly. "I'll bet Martin likes snow."

He had a mouth full of potatoes and nodded eagerly.

"I'd still like to know how you skate in snow," Ernie said, persistent, eyeing Bob in triumph.

"Go look it up in a book. Since you're so *interested,*" Elsie said, with a glance that indicated terrible things would happen to Ernie, later on.

Bob said, "Heh, heh, watch out Pop! You're gonna get it now!"

Doreen cried, "Bob! Mind your manners," and punched him in the shoulder.

Lyn screamed, "Skating! I wanna go skating!"

Ernie pretended he hadn't heard any of this. He had a pea stuck to the side of his cheek; it remained there while he continued chewing. He pulled a fish bone from his mouth.

"You've got a pea stuck on your face," Elsie said sharply.

"Good," Ernie said, grinning nastily. "Do you want it?" He grazed his cheek with his hand. The pea fell on the floor, and he winked at Martin, who was feeling right at home. That was the main thing as far as the rest of them were concerned. Forget about snow. Forget about Ernie and the stuck pea. Martin Defolio was winning all the points. He was acting like he belonged. His jacket was slung across the back of his chair; his sleeves were rolled up his skinny arms like he meant business; he'd loosened his tie. Martin was a "dear" and "a good egg" and an "all right guy." He was such a success that I had the sick feeling he'd be invited for Christmas dinner. There could be nothing worse.

"Martin," Elsie now said, "I hear you plan on being an accountant." When Martin looked dumbfounded, she pressed on. "Like Mr. Holt next door. He's an accountant. And very well off, too." She stared pointedly at Ernie while she spoke, meaning, we knew, "unlike *you* with your janitor's job."

"Huh?"

I held my breath.

"An accountant. Marion tells me you've got a head for figures."

"I bet he does," Bob cracked. "Eh, Marty? Va-va-va-voom." He pulled his shirt out from his chest. "Get a load of these knockers!"

"Oh, Bob," Doreen said wearily, "don't be such a moron."

"Voom voom," Lyn squealed.

Beside me Martin grinned at everyone and steadily pushed food into his mouth, including the salmon. Before long he choked on a fish bone. It seems he didn't know you weren't supposed to eat them. He coughed and coughed and his face turned red. Elsie jumped up and got a piece of bread and told him to swallow it, which he did, but not before Bob had given him several hard slaps on the back and Ernie had cried out, "Oh, heck!" and glanced, panic stricken, at the phone in the hall. "Shouldn't we call an ambulance?"

"Don't be bloody ridiculous," Elsie said, forgetting her company manners in the midst of the catastrophe. "The bread will work just fine."

After Martin had swallowed the bone everyone laughed and congratulated him. Ernie said, "We thought you were a goner." Elsie gave him some sliced peaches and ice cream and said, "You won't choke on this, dear."

Then we had tea, weak as usual, because Elsie could never wait to pour it.

Martin Defolio left after the *Ed Sullivan Show*, which started at eight. Everyone insisted he watch it with us. I couldn't wait for him to leave but I was outnumbered. Seven of us were squeezed into the den. Martin sat chummily on the couch beside Elsie. I sat on the floor next to Ernie's chair, and Lyn sat on Ernie's lap. Doreen grabbed kitchen chairs for her and Bob.

The show began. There were acrobats and jugglers and a comedian to watch; an opera singer in the audience who was told to stand up and take a bow; five minstrel singers in blackface singing "Old Black Joe;" the June Taylor Dancers lying on their backs making kaleidoscope designs with their legs. You watched them do this through a special camera mounted on the ceiling of the theatre. It was the highlight of the show. Then it was over.

At the door Martin said, "Jawannagooutfridaynight?"

"I suppose," I said.

"Getchaseven?"

"Might as well."

Then he pulled his ring off his finger.

"Wannagosteady?"

I gasped.

Martin grinned. "Jawanna?"

I took the ring, a gold "M" set in black onyx. It was

heavy. I could wear it on a chain around my neck like a trophy. Finally! All my girlfriends wore rings on chains, something that was a sore point with me; I was the only one who didn't. I'd wear the ring to school tomorrow, hanging outside my white sweater so everyone could see, a tiny hubcap banging triumphantly against my chest.

We kissed sloppily.

I pushed him away. "My aunt might see!"

Minutes later I was wailing down the phone line to my best friend, Dana.

"Mr. Puke gave me his ring!"

Dana squealed like this was the best news in the world.

The next day Elsie mentioned the baked salmon. "Dry as a popcorn fart," she said. "It was hardly touched. What a waste!" She gave me the evil eye.

"So much for Martin's special diet. Hah!" She put the salmon outside for the gulls.

TWO YEARS LATER, when Martin Defolio was ancient history, I got a summer job working in the kitchen at the Butchart's Gardens restaurant. There I learned from the Brentwood Bay farm women who were hired as summer cooks how to bake salmon. It's a simple recipe and the salmon is always moist.

When I tried the recipe for my family that summer Elsie picked at it. "Not bad," she allowed. "But then I've never been fond of fish. Must have been the fish heads my mother boiled for soup when I was a kid. The smell alone would kill you!"

Ernie agreed by asking the obvious: "Why would you want salmon when you can have roast beef?"

But I like it and use this recipe often.

Baked Salmon:
Whole salmon, Sockeye or Pink
Olive oil
Salt
Lemon slices

Fill cavity of salmon with lemon slices. Sprinkle with salt. Drizzle olive oil over inside and outside of fish. Wrap in tin foil. Bake in a 325 degree oven for fifteen minutes a pound.

YOUR HOME & YOU

MISS HORREL, our hefty grade 10 Home Ec teacher, was demonstrating how to sift flour. She stood before twenty girls, massive and inviolate in her handmade tweed suit with its handmade button holes, while outside the sun shone, plum trees blossomed, and sullen older boys waited for us in souped-up cars. It was the last period on a Friday afternoon.

Miss Horrel held the hand-cranked sifter over a sheet of wax paper and instructed us to turn to page ninety-one in our textbook, *Your Home & You*. Here she read aloud. "In using flour for quick breads, sift before measuring."

"Write that down, girls," Miss Horrel said. "And remember, the secret to light muffins is sifted flour." Then she paused to deliver her revelation. "Flour must be sifted not once, but *twice* if your muffins are to be light and airy! That's something you won't find in your textbooks." Which meant it would be a test question on the final exam. We wrote furiously.

It was 1963 and we all knew why we were there: we were housewives in training. Eventually a perfected version of Miss Horrel's muffins would land in the mouths of our shirt-and-tie husbands, perhaps even in the mouths of the Larrys, Als, and Pats who were waiting outside at that very moment.

Muffin-making was difficult work, *scientific* work, we were told, and a vitally important skill to conquer if we were to ever take our places as confident homemakers of the nation. There were the exact measurements of baking powder, sugar, flour, and milk to consider, the crucial element of a well-greased muffin tin; the importance of lumpy batter.

There were six work stations in Miss Horrel's class. Each station consisted of four girls seated around an Arborite-topped table. A bank of cupboards and drawers behind us were filled with our tools-in-trade—mixing bowls, muffin tins, cookie sheets, frying pans, and all manner of arcane utensils. We sat with our "Muffin Preparation Plans" before us and wore full, white aprons with our names embroidered across the bibs.

We had sewn these rights-of-passage aprons in grade 7 to mark the beginning of our domestic indoctrination. Ahead lay six years of learning increasingly difficult recipes, from Pea Soup in grade 7—*One can of peas, mashed, one cup of water, one cup milk, salt and pepper to taste. And make sure you use a double boiler so the milk doesn't scald*—to Macaroni and Cheese, Brown Betty, Poached Eggs in grades 8 and 9, and then on to the challenging shoulder-cuts of meat in the higher grades. Marriage after high school was, of course, the intended climax of these earnest years, when *Your Home & You* would become reality. Marriage would transform us, we understood, into the smiling, high-heeled blonde in the flowered apron that figured so prominently in our text books.

Miss Horrel droned on. "When is a muffin done? What

are the four tests? Lynne? Marion? Dana? Paulette?"

Consulting our books we read aloud, dutifully as opposed to sarcastically; there was no sense in irritating Miss Horrel on a Friday afternoon: "The colour should be golden brown." "The muffins should pull away from the pan." "When you touch the top of the muffin with your finger the dent should spring back." "A knitting needle or a toothpick inserted in the centre of the muffin should come out clean."

Satisfied with our answers she instructed us to write that down as well.

MUFFIN WAS A WORD we used to mean small tits so it was hard to keep a straight face during Miss Horrel's demonstration. Using a kind of Home Ec Canadian standard format we graded our breasts the same way we had learned to grade eggs—from the smallest to the largest: "fried eggs," "muffins," "grapefruits," climaxing at the coveted "basket-balls," meaning you were so stacked a boy's eyes fell out of his head when you passed by. Only one of my school friends had that distinction—the envied Paulette. Dana, Lynne, and I were solid muffins with maybe a slim chance of becoming grapefruits in later years. Miss Horrel had basketballs, but, being a teacher, we didn't admire them.

School was Royal Oak Junior High. Grades 8 to 10; two hundred sixty-three kids; thirteen teachers. Most of the men teachers were ex-military. The three women on staff—Home Ec, English, Typing—were unmarried. The school served a wide area—the farmlands of Central Saanich, the suburbs of Royal Oak, and Cordova Bay, three miles away. The school itself was made of cement blocks and set in a gully. In winter the gully became a swamp and the cafeteria flooded. We called the school Royal Joke.

MISS HORREL'S FIANCÉ had been killed in World War 2 and it was understood that she would remain husband-less forever. She was in her mid-forties then and we pitied her. She would never know the ecstasy of serving a perfect muffin to an appreciative husband, would never be the wife of any house, and, worse, would have to eat her muffins by herself, getting fatter and fatter as the lonely years crept by.

"Always a bridesmaid, never a bride," Elsie said of her sadly. But there was a hint of disgust in her voice. Obviously Miss Horrel was remiss in not tackling her situation more clear-sightedly. By pining for lost love, she had willfully and foolishly ruined her chances. "She could have found *someone*," Elsie said, as if spare men were waiting by the side of the road for Miss Horrel to drive by and pick them up.

"There's lots of single men still living with their mothers who would appreciate a woman like Miss Horrel, a good cook and homemaker," Elsie said. "Think what her old age will be like all alone. Always a fifth wheel at family dinners. Tagging along on drives." She shuddered.

"But isn't that how you got Ernie?" I asked. "Wasn't he a spare man living with his mother? Across the street from Grandma and Auntie Maudie's house?"

"Not the same thing! I was a widow with two small girls *and* I was on welfare. Son's family never lifted a finger to help," she added bitterly. "And Ernie had a steady job at the library and said he'd build me a house. And that's what every woman wants. A home of her own. And I got one."

"Oh."

"But what's the big deal," she scoffed, "about Miss Horrel and those muffins? Dry old things. Even the seagulls won't touch 'em." Elsie's expertise was brownies and lemon squares and double-crusted pies.

Despite Miss Horrel's grim domestic life, she was an enthusiast for housewifery, something we could never countenance given her old maid status.

"Go figger!" we'd say to each another. If you couldn't have *Your Home & You* as your very own reality, what was the point of menu planning? Of living? Why not kill yourself and be done with it?

MISS HORREL, like Elsie, was a maniac for cleaning, and this was also something she taught. In those days garbage may have been thrown out of car windows with abandon, but the ideal home was spotless. From Miss Horrel we learned the secret of removing grime from walls, cupboards, and bathtubs— ammonia and dish soap—and how to scrub a floor on your hands and knees using vinegar and scalding hot water. We learned to use Lysol on toilets and sinks; spray Raid along baseboards in all seasons except winter; put perfume on dust rags so they would always smell sweet; and cover a broom with a dishtowel to sweep the ceiling for cobwebs. Not a speck of dust, not a scurrying bug, she told us, was allowed to take up residence in our future homes. We should, she said, be able to eat off our floors.

It sounded like slavery to me. I couldn't get over the fact that, as a future wife, I was expected to do all this—work. And not once in a while, but day in day out, for years. This was what having a home of one's own meant? Eternal drudgery?

Elsie's housekeeping followed the spotless dictum, as did Mrs. Holt's next door, and Doreen's, and the houses of my girlfriends. They were part of the war-on-germs obsession that had overtaken women in the Western world. Every household that I knew of was run along these lines. That is, except for

Auntie Maudie's house. Hers was a testament to benign neglect, and in my mind she was a heroine and a rebel.

I loved that she let things in her fridge go mouldy; that milk got left out and soured, that canned peaches exploded in her basement; that dust gathered like tumbleweed beneath her bed; and that cobwebs covered the Aspidistra. When Elsie would tartly point out her housekeeping faults, Maudie would shrug her shoulders and laugh. She was too busy to bother, she'd say. There was the crossword puzzle to do, or her roses to tend to. There were letters to write to girlfriends in England that she hadn't seen in forty years, or family pictures to sort through, or an interesting article in *Reader's Digest* to look at. Even though there were holes in her stockings and threads hanging from her skirt hem, I admired the fact that other things were more important to her than housekeeping. Maudie's example meant that all the down-on-your-knees sweat over the kitchen floor that Elsie performed like a martyr—"No one appreciates the work I do!"—the constant mania about spots on the glasses, the windows, on your face, the way women lived in servitude to cleanliness, how it overtook their lives, was really not that important. Maudie proved this. Her house seemed fine to me. It was a celebration of barely controlled chaos. And, more importantly, Maudie was always happy. Hers was a relaxed household, more comfortable to be in than the usual spotless houses because you didn't have to constantly worry about where you put your glass, or if your shoes were wiped. At Maudie's house crumbs were scattered on the floors like confetti.

SOME OF US made notes that day while Miss Horrel talked—Monday would be the actual muffin-making day—and some of us watched the institutional clock on the wall.

Miss Horrel was also our Guidance teacher and she had recently told us that it only took four minutes for a boy to destroy a girl's life. I wondered how she, being an old virgin, would know the specific time.

I'd watched the institutional clock on the wall above her desk after she'd made this announcement: the red second hand, the heavy minute hand, and the eternity they took to round the circle. Four minutes is a long time. I'd always thought your life would be ruined in an instant, if you drowned say, or were bashed on the head. But Miss Horrel said four minutes; she was definite about this. Would the four minutes include kissing beforehand and the rumoured shared cigarette when it was all over?

It wasn't hard to picture Miss Horrel peering through a steamed-up car window at Mt. Doug on a Friday night with her Sports Day stopwatch at the ready to time the four-minute dash: "Wait. Wait. Begin timing. Now!"

YEARS LATER, Miss Horrel and her homemaking advice are still with me—in spite of my early resistance to it. Because, as it turned out, having a home of my own was something I really did want. Though its cleanliness has never reached Miss Horrel's—or Elsie's—standard, it has become like Maudie's. Thankfully, Miss Horrel and high school Home Ec have come to my domestic rescue many times over the years, especially with her recipes for cheap and nutritious soups—boiled bones and vegetables—and the many things you can do with eggs. Her training in thrift has stood me well because, as it turned out, my husband and I were frequently broke. And, surprisingly, I find housecleaning to be a calming activity. There are times when, like Elsie, I would rather scrub a wall than have a conversation. Women didn't have yoga in her and Miss Horrel's day. But, actually, scrubbing a wall amounts to the same thing.

VICTORIA'S ONLY TOE-TAPPER

WHEN I WAS FIFTEEN I was billed as Victoria's only toe-tapper. This may or may not have been true. It was announced with three exclamation marks in Miss Blythe's dance recital programme. "Three exclamation marks!!!" I told my friends. "I'm famous!"

Towards the end of the second act of *Stars of Tomorrow* the curtain closed and the Billy Tickle Orchestra in the pit at the Royal Theatre in Victoria played the opening bars of "Shuffle Off to Buffalo." This was my cue. Dressed in black satin shorts, a matching tuxedo jacket, black fishnet stockings, and a top hat Elsie had made out of cardboard and had painted black, I began my routine, a novelty act in front of the curtain while the stage behind was being prepared for the finale, an extravaganza number involving the entire dance school called "Holiday in Rio."

My pointe shoes had special taps affixed to the toes so that toe-tapping was like dancing on stilts. The routine consisted of pounding and hopping movements, several turns, and a couple of "breaks," which was a difficult step to do on your toes—one leg kicked back while balancing on the other. I thought I heard the audience gasp when I did the first one but the sound might have been Miss Blythe hissing at me from the wings. Throughout my performance she kept up a steady prompt—"Smile, godammit, smile!"

Smiling while dancing, Miss Blythe often said, was personality, and personality would win the audience over every time.

Because of the lighting I couldn't see the audience—beyond the stage it was solid blackness—so it was hard to tell if my hopeful smiling was winning anyone over. The dance itself was like performing on the edge of a void, like grinning into nothingness, something a friend says I now do a lot in my writing, akin to whistling in the dark.

That evening I proceeded on faith; somewhere out there Elsie, Ernie, and my father Billy were watching, maybe even thinking I was the next Judy Garland.

I loved tap dancing—the regular kind—the speed and abandoning fun of it. There was nothing like tapping to "Sweet Georgia Brown," played robustly by the pianist, the elderly Irene, in the practice room at Miss Blythe's downtown studio. Five or six of us gleefully rehearsing the number while Irene, sweating at the keyboard, cheered us on: "That's it, girls! Now you're ripping up the boards!"

I'd been attending Miss Blythe's dance school for six years by the time I was singled out for toe-tapping stardom. She'd liked me well enough when I was younger and had long blonde hair—she preferred her girls to look like fairy princesses—but at thirteen when it was cut short I was relegated to the back row in all the production numbers, to the no-girls-land where the inept, the unlovely, and the overweight were hidden. It was therefore a shock when she plucked me from dancing obscurity and had me fitted for toe-taps. I wondered if she was punishing me in some way.

She was a demanding teacher and, to my mind, a ghoulish one. She seemed to like nothing better than pitting one girl against another; tears and hysteria were common features of her classes. "If you can't stand the heat get off the dance floor," she'd holler at some sobbing girl who'd just been told she pirouetted like a hippo. The admired girls were the ones with waist-length hair who half-fainted from overexertion and had to be helped to the bathroom where they could vomit demurely. These fainting girls, Miss Blythe told us, were examples of what "trying harder" meant.

She was in her fifties at the time of (what turned out to be) my one and only toe-tapping performance. A slim woman with tightly curled brown hair, she wore black pants, a black turtleneck, and ballerina slippers during our tap and ballet lessons. The rhinestones attached to the wingtips of her glasses gave off a malevolent glint when caught by the overhead lights. It was rumoured she'd once danced on Broadway, though Elsie sniffed when she heard this. "Show me the pictures! Where's the proof?"

In "real life," Elsie noted, Miss Blythe was a sad and lonely widow who lived by herself in a big empty house on the Dallas Road waterfront. Furthermore, she had no children. "Her students are her children," Elsie said. "The poor thing."

Miss Blythe chain-smoked through our lessons, roaming the practice room with her cigarette and ashtray like a stalker on the lookout for bent backs and knock knees. "Stand up! Toes out!" she'd cry, then wheeze and cough. Amazingly, she lived to be a hundred.

WHILE MY TOE-TAPPING SOLO was nothing to write home about, as Elsie later remarked, Miss Blythe must have decided that I possessed enough "personality" to become one of her passing favourites because shortly after the recital she put forth Sherry's, Nadine's, and my name to the Victoria Celebrations Society. They were looking for three girls with "character" to help promote Victoria's centennial. The three of us were to visit up-Island towns for ten days at the beginning of August— it was billed as a "goodwill tour"—with "Victoria's first mayor," a man in his sixties called Sparky McFadden who'd be playing the part. Before that we were to sell centennial booster buttons on the streets of Victoria during the month of July.

The contract we signed with the Victoria Celebrations Society said we would be paid five dollars a day plus meals and accommodation for the trip, and twenty percent of all proceeds from the button sales, meaning we'd make five cents for every twenty-five-cent button we sold.

The Celebrations Society was housed in an empty store on Douglas Street next to People's Credit Jewellers. Inside there were only two tables, two chairs, two phones, and two crewcut guys called Gary and Hank who were running things.

We were called "The Ambassadorettes" and outfitted at Tip Top Tailors with red velvet tuxedo jackets and grey flannel pants. I was allowed to go on the trip because it was "an official job," and because Miss Blythe had recommended me.

We didn't meet Sparky McFadden until the morning of the up-Island trip. I had sold three hundred and thirty-six booster buttons by then, earning a paltry sixteen dollars and eighty cents.

Sparky was a small man with a florid face and a short white beard which, as he made a point of telling us, was real.

"Here," he said frequently, "pull it." This was something, I discovered in later years, that many men were fond of saying.

Sparky wore an old-time mayor's costume and a black top hat. It was his car we'd be travelling in, a 1954 green Ford.

Before we left, Gary—he looked like Bobby Darrin—took me aside and gave me a fifty-dollar bill. "You look like the ringleader," he told me. "This is in case you get into trouble." Puzzled, I took the money.

For the first two days things were okay. As an official delegation we visited the Chamber of Commerce in Duncan and then dropped in on a woman's one-hundredth birthday party. It was happening at the Kiwanis Centre where a lot of people were standing around holding teacups. The old woman was sitting in an armchair decorated with twisted green and yellow crepe paper, the kind of decoration done for bridal showers. When she saw the four of us in our costumes striding towards her she got scared and cried. We stayed long enough to have our pictures taken with her for the Duncan paper. The headline, when we saw it, read, "Two Centennials."

Between events, Sherry, Nadine and I lounged in the back seat of Sparky's Ford, he driving up front like a chauffeur. We lined our top hats in a row on the ledge behind the seat and shared movie magazines and comics and sang along to Motown hits on my transistor radio. I used part of the fifty dollars the organizer had given me to buy us potato chips, *Cheezies,* and bags of scotch mints and jelly beans. We screamed at Sparky to stop for fries and cokes every time we passed a coffee shop or a drive-in.

From our motel in Nanaimo, Sparky dropped us off at a movie—*Elmer Gantry*—and took himself to a bar.

The next morning, day three, we were on our way to Campbell River when Sparky began openly drinking rye from a brown paper bag. He said we were driving him nuts. All our squealing and singing and talk about movie stars and makeup and hairdos was driving him "stark, raving bonkers."

"You sound like a bunch of crazed chickens. Squawk, squawk, squawk,"said Sparky McFadden.

"You do that good," I said. "You sound like a rooster. Like an *old* rooster."

This made us laugh and start singing loudly—"*They say that breaking up is har-ard to do-oo...*"

"I should have known," Sparky McFadden said, pulling at his beard, and then guzzling from the paper bag.

"*Now I know. Know that it's tru-oo...Breaking up is...har-ard to do-oou...*"

Around 11 o'clock he pulled over and turned to us. He was grinning and waving his fingers.

"Bye, bye," he slurred, and passed out across the seat.

For a while we sat there stunned and watched him snore. Then we felt disgusted.

"What a puke," I said, not knowing that puke in the form of Martin Defolio would soon become a big part of my life.

"Just a cruddy old drunk," said Nadine, who was a good tap dancer and could sing on stage like a cowgirl—"*I'm an old cow hand...from the Rio Grande...*"

"What shall we doooooo?" Sherry moaned. She was known for her back flips and the splits; "She's made of rubber," people said, awed. I, of course, was Victoria's Only Toe-Tapper (say no more).

Cars sped by. None of us could drive. Sherry was the oldest at seventeen but she didn't have her license. Nadine was fifteen, the same age as me. There was nowhere to phone.

"So what's the big deal?" I said, and climbed over the seat. I shoved Sparky's legs out of the way and started the engine. But didn't know how to use the clutch or change gears. The car kept stalling. Finally I managed to lurch along in first. The car felt huge—what I imagined riding bareback on a bull would be like—wide and unwieldy. I drove mostly on the shoulder and then, gaining confidence pulled onto the road—still in first gear—and got the speed up to thirty. But when a car passed I panicked, and swerved right, jerking to a stop down a ditch. The car shuddered, then wheezed. The top half of Sparky rolled onto the floor. He didn't wake up.

"Quick," I said. "Before someone comes."

We pulled and shoved him back onto the seat and propped him behind the steering wheel. Then we stood on the highway in our high heels and top hats. A woman driving by—"Oh, you poor things!"—took us to the police station where we were told we were lucky to escape with our lives. I used what was left of the fifty dollars for our bus ride home.

We told our families that Sparky got sick and the trip was cancelled.

But that was the end of "Victoria's first mayor" and the Ambassadorettes.

LATER THAT SUMMER Elsie, Maudie, Grandma, Elsie's daughters Doreen and Shirley, and Victoria's Only Toe-Tapper were sitting outside on the front patio facing the traffic of Cordova Bay Road. All of us, except Grandma, were wearing muumuus. It was the season of the muumuu, that baggy, shape-hiding dress from Hawaii.

Shirley had arrived two days earlier from Sunnyvale, California, for a three-week holiday. She was twenty-five years old at the time and seven-months pregnant with her third child. But you'd never know it because of the orange-flowered muumuu she was wearing. Unlike ours, which Elsie had made, Shirley's muumuu was store-bought and of a superior design and fabric. She looked sophisticated in her American clothes, big town, and wore sandals of a style we'd never seen before and now coveted—cork wedgies with the toes covered in pink plastic flowers.

Of the two sisters, Shirley was always referred to as the spunky one, the daredevil. Four years younger than Doreen, she had red hair and freckles. This feature, Elsie said, was the cause of Shirley's spunkiness and the reason she had "a mind of her own," meaning she did what she liked. As far as I understood, this was mainly to quit school at sixteen, marry young, move to California, and have all those kids, four things I vowed would never happen to me.

Unlike Shirley, no one ever called *me* spunky, so perhaps I needn't have worried. I was "Miss Priss," and "Pus Lips" (white lipstick), names that rendered me happily immune, I believed, from quitting school and marrying early. On top of this, Elsie often hooted, "Who'd want to marry you? Boys want nice girls. Not someone who traipses around with her nose stuck in the air like you do."

It seemed I was my family's version of *The Taming of the Shrew* because Elsie would invariably add with glee, "You just wait. You'll get knocked down to size."

That afternoon on the patio Maudie was sitting quietly nearby and paying warm and benevolent witness to the splendour that was the rest of us, as she always did. We counted on her seeing us this way. You could only be wonderful in Maudie's eyes because Maudie loved everyone. Which was a fault, Elsie said, especially when it came to Frank, her long-dead husband, and her only son, Kenny Pepper, who was twenty-nine, unemployed, and still lived at home. He was, Elsie said, what Maudie lived for.

"But he doesn't appreciate what she does for him," Elsie would always add righteously. "Won't get out of bed till 3 in the afternoon. Poor Maudie has to lug the garbage cans to the end of the driveway herself. And don't even get me started on the way she waits on him hand and foot!"

For this reason we felt sorry for Maudie. She may have been a saint, but she clearly suffered in silence, the only dignified thing a woman could do. This silent suffering was the truth, Elsie said. It explained Maudie's continual smiling. She smiled to hide her pain.

That day, Maudie was smiling as usual. She was wearing a muumuu that had purple flowers on a hot pink background. Elsie had made it for her birthday because Maudie would never sew a muumuu for herself. Housedresses, cardigans, and oxford shoes were what she wore. Elsie, however, deemed it one of her many missions in life to educate her dowdy sister about style. You were supposed to wear rubber thongs or high heels, or, like Shirley, wedged sandals, with a muumuu but Maudie would not. She couldn't be persuaded to give up her black oxfords; she wore them with her muumuu without stockings. Her bare legs were disgracefully white, with gnarly dark varicose veins wandering across her shins, and her feet had bunions, as Elsie's did, lumps of bone and flesh sticking out below their big toes which probably explained why they hobbled when they walked.

Elsie looked at Maudie and sighed—it was hopeless!— and exchanged eye-rolling looks with Doreen and Shirley. But Maudie seemed oblivious to this. On the patio that day she was sitting on her hands, swinging her short legs, and beaming at us. We're wonderful, her shining eyes told us, too wonderful for words.

Shirley was lounging on one of Ernie's homemade deck chairs alongside Doreen. She was in a bad mood. Tired, she said. "I could sleep for a whole bloody year," she yawned. She sounded like Elsie; there was that edge. Her children, Susan and Jimmy, aged four and three, were playing in the new sandbox on the grass beside the patio. Doreen's three-year-old daughter Lyn was with them. They had pails and shovels and, for the moment, were quiet; no whining or crying came from their direction and it was blissful.

All these little kids, I was thinking, watching them with dismay. It was all anyone ever talked about. They were cute, all right, I gave them that, but I hated babysitting them. I hated babysitting period. I was not one of those teenage girls driven to child care. I was never going to have children. From what I could see it was all work and no fun. And marriage was even worse. I was sitting there, considering these things while painting my nails. I had plenty of examples to judge from, I continued, musing. Shirley's marriage, for starters. Her husband Ken hadn't come on this trip; he'd stayed in California. Everyone was glad about this because Ken was a shouter. He shouted at his kids—just babies!—and he shouted at Shirley. Also he drank. He was a bartender so he drank, that was the explanation. I thought Ken was mean and wished Shirley had never married him. Now I was hoping she'd leave him and move back home. I'd put up with the kids just to have her here. I'd make myself stand it for Shirley's sake.

Elsie was talking about this very subject, something she'd been doing non-stop since Shirley arrived. "Move back home," she urged her again. "Ernie'll fix up the basement. You can stay here. Till you get settled."

But Shirley was giving her an argument. "How would I live? The baby's due in November. I can't go out to work."

"You can get welfare," Elsie said. "I did. When your father was in the sanitarium I didn't have a choice. I made do with thirty-seven dollars and fifty cents a month. And the family will help."

I gave a laugh.

"What's so funny?" Elsie said. "Think you're too good for us?" She turned to the others. "Gets a toe-tap solo and thinks she's the Queen of bloody Sheba."

"Thirty-seven dollars and fifty cents. Big deal," I said. "What could you buy with that?"

"It was plenty. You don't know what you're talking about."

"Excuse me," Shirley butted in, peeved. "I *have* a choice. About moving back. Ken's got a steady job and he says he'll stop drinking. Besides, I like it in Sunnyvale."

"You like those friends of yours," Elsie snapped. "Barb and Bob. They're not your family. They won't be there for you when things get tough."

"Things won't get tough," Shirley said.

"How can you stand Ken?" I added. "The way he screams at everyone."

My comment hung in the air, fizzing out by the second. No one was interested in what I had to say. Elsie and Shirley were the stars of this conversation.

And it had clearly gone on long enough because Elsie next loaded and fired her biggest gun. "Well, you'll never see Grandma again if you stay in California. She'll be dead by the time you decide to move back."

Shirley looked at her mother in horror.

"See if I'm not right," Elsie said. "She's eighty-eight years old. How much longer do you think she's got?" The oracle had spoken

Doreen, the beautiful *and* the sensitive one, started crying. Grandma was sitting on a kitchen chair in the shade of the carport roof staring at the road and counting the cars going by. She turned to us and said, "Thirty-two," and Doreen let out a sob. Maudie shrugged her shoulders and looked hopeless; Shirley scowled at her mother; Victoria's Only Toe-Tapper applied another coat of Pink Pearl nail polish. Only Elsie, having rested her case, looked pleased.

I was wondering, "What now?" when one of the kids screamed. Sand had been thrown, or one of them had fallen, or one of them had messed their pants. It was always something; you never knew the cause. But the howling was the same. And contagious. One cried, they all cried.

Later, when things had settled down—food given, different toys offered—and we were having tea, Elsie came up with a bright idea. "I know," she exclaimed. "Let's go shopping!"

In an instant I saw what was coming and started gathering up my nail polish things.

"What we need is a trip to Town and Country Mall," Elsie said. "That'll cheer everyone up. There's a sale of towels on at Woolworth's! And Ingledew's is having a shoe sale!" To Maudie she said, "You love a sale, don't you? We can drop you and Ma home on the way back."

But I'm not invited. I'm needed to babysit.

"Sorry," I said, getting up. "I'm busy."

"We'll pay you," Doreen hastily offered.

"No," I said, glowering at her. "Wild horses couldn't make me."

"Oh, please," Doreen begged. "Shirley won't be here for long. It'll be a treat for her to get away from the kids. We'll only be gone a couple of hours."

"I told you I'm busy. I'm going down the beach." I headed into the house to get my towel.

Behind me Elsie hollered, "There she goes: Victoria's One and Only—Pain in the Ass."

I turned around. Everyone looked gloomy. Then one of

the kids screamed. Over the howling, Maudie said, "Oh well, maybe it's a phase."

"Phase, my eye," Elsie snorted. "Doreen and Shirley were never this bad. They always did what they were told in the end."

"Until now," Shirley said.

part 2
LATER

SKIDNEY

NANA, MY MOTHER-IN-LAW who lives with Terry and me and our teenage kids, plays bridge Wednesday nights at the Sidney Silver Threads. She's usually home by 10 but this week she came through the door at 8:45. Came into our bedroom, flushed and excited, and announced, "They evacuated the Centre! Gas leak!"

This was better than any disaster show on TV.

"There were sixteen tables of bridge," she told us, "and suddenly we could smell gas. Howard, the director, called the fire department and then asked the players: 'You can either carry on with the bridge game or you can go home. What do you want to do?' And everyone yelled in one voice, 'Play bridge!'"

When I heard this I immediately wrote the *National Enquirer* headline: "Seniors Elect To Play Bridge in Death Trap."

And why wouldn't they? When you're eighty, or ninety, why not play bridge in the midst of a potential explosion? It makes sense: it's a chance to go out with a literal bang. Possibly the last chance. And it's the opposite of those sad people who quit smoking a week before they die of lung cancer or who abandon their daily ration of cinnamon buns and take up weight training at age eighty-eight.

But the bridge players' thrill had been short-lived. A fireman dressed in a yellow and black rubber suit and yellow helmet, with an oxygen tank strapped to his back, stood at the doorway to the bridge room and bellowed, "Evacuate! Now!"

"It was so exciting," Nana said. "Outside there were fire trucks and police cars with their lights flashing. And the road on either side of the Centre was closed off with that yellow tape you see on the news. What they use when there's a murder."

THIS IS ABOUT as exciting as Sidney gets.

True, there's the Sidney Days Parade on July 1st followed by the giant sidewalk sale down Beacon Avenue. And there's the Santa Claus Parade where local businessmen attach helium-filled balloons to their minivans and holler at the shivering crowd, "Ten percent off blinds at *Fashion Focus Paint & Accessories*!"

But exciting?

This year the Santa Claus parade included Bill's band playing live music from the back of a flatbed truck. They had seven blocks in which to impress the crowd. When they passed by us, the band was in the pause between songs. What we got was some amp noise. Seven blocks goes by fast even at the pace of a parade. My husband only got one blurred picture of our son's back while he was tuning his guitar.

The band's other guitarist took thirty minutes off work

at The Pantry, where he's a short-order cook, so he could be in the parade. How small town, I thought. I pictured him throwing off his greasy apron and running out of the restaurant at the last moment. Climbing onto the back of the truck as it began the parade and hastily donning his denim rock-star hat and carefully ripped jacket for his instant identity change.

It's like the volunteer fire department. The man who's filling your tank at the gas station could, moments after the alarm sounds, be the same man hanging off the back of a wailing fire truck.

SIDNEY REALLY IS a small town—a small town on a largish island. The main street, Beacon Avenue, veers off the Pat Bay Highway, a four-lane road whose main purpose is to link Victoria with the Swartz Bay Terminal and the ferries to Vancouver. Day and night, cars scream past Sidney. You can picture the panicked ferry-goers clawing at their car windows. "A cute island, yes, but let us off RIGHT NOW!!"

Take a breath, you want to call, there'll be lineups, delays, and what's so great about Vancouver? This is much the same message Sidney's town officials have tried to convey. Hoping to share in the tourist money that Victoria attracts, they've spiffed the place up with paving-stone sidewalks and nautical-style street signs. A billboard on the highway before you reach the town announces hopefully: "Welcome to Beautiful Sidney by the Sea."

Those of us who live in or around Sidney agree it's a beautiful place. But many of us are glad the tourists largely ignore the town—we like it quiet and dull—and wish the officials would cease their relentless advertising campaigns. It's embarrassing. It's pathetic. It's like the time when I was fourteen years old and travelling in Oregon State with my family. Driving through a small town, we passed a rundown motel. A woman wearing an apron and a girl about my age rushed out from the motel and stopped our car. They looked desperate. "Please," the woman said. "Stay here! We'll give you a really good rate."

My father couldn't drive away fast enough.

SIDNEY'S TOWN OFFICIALS are trying to make Sidney into a travel destination. But you wonder if there really are excited families in Montana or Manitoba or Japan or New York planning a dream vacation to Sidney. This is just not a place you save up and travel to. Maybe, if the weather's good, you stop in for an hour or two on your way from Victoria to the ferry, poke around the nautical theme shops and Tanner's Books and maybe take a stroll along the newly invented Port Sidney to look at the boats. But you won't stay here for long. Where's the theme park? Where's the mall? Where's the world's largest stuffed salmon?

OUR KIDS' NAME for Sidney is Skidney. A place light years away from the town inhabited by the handful of writers, the well-heeled retirees, the young families saving up for a starter home.

When I hear the word Skidney I naturally think of Skid Row, a despairing place filled with drunks, addicts, and the homeless. But what the kids mean by Skidney is that it's a rough, down-home, beer-drinking, unpretentious place. Bill's nineteen, Anna's sixteen, and so is Kristy, Anna's best friend whom we're fostering, and to them Skidney is a state of mind.

"IN SKIDNEY, when you go to a party," Bill told me, "you hold onto your beer. Actually hold onto it. There's all these kids standing around talking or they're dancing and they'll have cases of beer stuck under their arms. No one's crazy enough to put them down because they'll get taken. So the thing is, you hold onto them no matter what. A lot of girls wear packs and put their beer in there. People at Skidney parties are always coming up to you and trying to bum a beer. You look in your case and say, 'Hey man, I've only got eight left. Sorry.' If you put your beer down even for a minute, it's gone. That's Skidney."

ANNA OFFERS her version of Skidney:

"There was this hard-core Barbie chick and she's like in the bowling alley with Mike Panowski. And she's supposedly his new girlfriend from Victoria? And I couldn't believe it. She thinks I'm hot on Mike because we're talking and it's weird how every time it's my turn to bowl it's his turn too. But I mean, like, Mike? Duh. But this Barbie chick keeps staring at me. Like a serious, big-time, jealousy trip. She's got these platform shoes on and tight black pants and perfect, wispy little bits of blonde hair pulled out of her ponytail. And she finally says to Mike before they've even finished their game, 'C'mon Mike, like, we're leaving.' And then she comes over to our table, all fake smiles and puts this half pitcher of beer in front of me and says, 'Like here, you can have this.' And we're like, wow thanks, that's really cool! And it took Charlotte and me half an hour to figure it out. We were supposed to be insulted. Like in the Barbie chick's world this was an insulting thing to do. And it was such a laugh. Because in our world, in Skidney, this is the coolest thing you can do. Hey, you want to give us some free beer? Right on!"

I GREW UP in Cordova Bay, some ten miles down the road from Sidney. A place our kids refer to as "preppy."

"Kids in Cordova Bay blow dry their hair and wear Fashions," Bill tells me disgustedly. "And they don't drink beer. At parties everyone puts their wine on the kitchen counter like grown-ups. When kids from Skidney go to one of their parties? The wine's gone in seconds."

WHEN I WAS a brawling young person, my friends and I often went "slumming" at the Sidney Hotel. We'd drink beer and watch the fights in the Beer Parlor, a large, noisy, brightly lit, smoky room filled with small round tables covered in red terry cloth. Each table had as many glasses of beer as it could hold—twenty or thirty glasses—and beer cost twenty-five cents a glass. Around 11 or 12 in the evening there'd always be a drunken fight or two, and the police would come. My Cordova Bay friends and I imagined we were seeing the wild side of life, and it was thrilling.

"That's nothing," Kristy said when she heard this story. "A couple of fights? Like, how protected!"

LAST HALLOWEEN my husband drove seven costumed girls to a party up the road. The girls weren't actually invited but it was "cool" because they knew someone who knew someone who was having the party. It was an outdoors party and you had to wear a costume.

Seven girls piled into the back of our pickup: a clown, a spider, a hooker, a Hawaiian in a pink wig, a New Age guru in a blue wig and white gown, a nymph wearing a crown of leaves, and a Raggedy Ann. Their packs bulged with cans of beer.

As they were pulling out of the driveway, one of the girls

yelled to my husband, "Do you mind if I light this?"

Terry, glancing in the rear-view mirror, saw what he thought was a monster joint. "Yes!" he croaked, sweat forming on his upper lip. It turned out to be a Roman candle.

"Lighting *that* would have been even worse," he said when he returned home. He also said, "I can't believe I did that. Driving seven minors in possession of alcohol in the back of my truck. Thank Christ the police were busy searching delinquents for dope at the community bonfire."

"YOU GO TO a Skidney party," Bill tells us, "and by 10 o'clock most everyone's drunk and puking, drunk and screaming, or passed out."

"Sounds like the good old days to me," Terry says.

For a year or two before I met him, Terry was a regular at the Sidney Hotel. There are guys he drank with then who are still hanging around the local bars on a full-time basis. Guys who never went anywhere. In their forties and fifties now, they're either on welfare or working part-time in construction. If it's summer, maybe stripping boats at one of the local marinas. Their backs are gone, their knees are gone, and if they ever had them, so are their families. The thing is: *they never got out of Sidney.*

Never getting out of Sidney is something our kids fear. What I hope they mean by this is: never getting beyond being what they call "a boozing loser."

We stayed in Sidney, Terry and me, so in a sense we never got out, either. But then we moved on, I tell the kids, *in other ways.* "It doesn't matter where you live. What matters is how you look at things, how you *experience* your lives."

They get quiet when I talk like this. They don't want to think ten years down the road. They want to think *tomorrow.*

And maybe the day after that—Friday night! They want to believe right now will last forever.

And what I believe is: What else is there to do with youth but spend it fast?

WE LIVE IN THE Deep Cove area of Sidney. There's a small beach at the foot of our hill where, in summer, Terry and I swim with our dog Mutz in the late afternoons. When the kids were small, before "Skidney" ever existed for us, they swam there, too. Those were years of riding on logs in the water and building castles on the sandbar, of seaweed fights and water-skiing behind a neighbour's boat. And running up the hill late for supper, their beautiful suntanned bodies covered in fine grey sand. Then flinging their inner tubes, their masks and snorkels, their wet towels onto the deck. Hosing themselves off before racing inside.

Now there's a new generation of young kids doing the same thing. And everyone down at the beach knows all the connections: whose kid belongs to whom and where, exactly, they live. And isn't it great, everyone says, that Kira's grandmother at eighty-two still swims every day?

The main topic of conversation amongst the swimmers has never changed: water temperature. "How's the water today?" You might ask this of someone who's just toweling off. What you'll hear is anything from "Beautiful!" to "Freezing. It'll make your bones ache."

Over the years, we've learned to tell the temperature of the water just by looking at it. Clear means cold; cloudy means warm. And the warmest water is when it has a greenish-brown tinge to it, an algae bloom. We're always telling dubious newcomers, "No, that's *not* pollution. It's a red tide. The swimming will be great!"

More than once, Stan, a wiry senior citizen who lives in a waterfront house, has bounded down the beach when he sees us taking our shoes off and arranging our towels on the sand. When he makes such a determined visit, we know what he's going to say. "Hey there, folks," he'll call a good fifty feet before he reaches us," did you hear that teenage party down here last night?"

"No!" we'll say, acting shocked by the very idea. We know he suspects our kids. But we want him to think they spend every waking moment volunteering at the hospital or attending Bible camp or walking the dogs of invalids.

Once, he'd asked about another party. "It was coming from up your way," he said, jerking his head in the direction of our house. "The music was so loud. All we could hear was this thumping sound. Thump. Thump. Thump."

"Must have been my mother," Terry had said brazenly. "She had a few of the ladies in for bridge last night. Must have put on Frank Sinatra. She's eighty-five but you know how these old girls like to party!"

"Hah! Eighty-five you say? Golly!"

It was, of course, *our* party and fourteen of our friends ripping up the carpet to the house sounds of Bob Sinclair.

About the teenage beach party, Stan pressed on. "You didn't hear it?" he asked, incredulous. "That surprises me. The music was so LOUD. And there was yelling and girls in the water screaming. You didn't hear it up your place?"

"We must have slept through it," Terry said, bored, and picked up a stick for the dog. The dog, excited, turning in circles across the sand to the water.

"Gosh, it was loud," Stan continued. "I would have thought you'd hear it at your house. No? I was down here this morning picking up empty beer bottles. Some of them broken. The garbage they left! I picked up half a dozen empty chip bags and cigarette packs. "

"Wasn't that good of you?" I said and my husband shot me a glance.

"Yes, well. At 10:30 I called the RCMP. Can you believe this? They couldn't come because of a house party in Sidney. Got out of control."

After Stan left to fling himself in the water and float on his back, Terry, pretending not to talk to me, stared at the water and whispered out the side of his mouth, "Where were they last night?"

"At a house party in Sidney," I replied, gazing placidly at the tiny windsurfers in the distance. Then added, "But not at the rowdy one. Another one."

Terry sighed. "So it wasn't *them* down here."

"No."

"I'm getting tired of Stan," my husband said.

THAT DAY WE WENT for our usual swim. Gently parting the seaweed as we breaststroked along the shore, the dog beside us. The water was "Fantastic!" "Beautiful!" "Like soup!" A few swimmers on the beach were stretched out on their towels, drying off in the sun. Toddlers and their older brothers and sisters played with plastic boats at the water's edge.

While over in Skidney our kids were having a respite from paradise, tearing up the town with their awful young lives.

DAY SHIFT

For Sara Dowse

FIFTEEN MINUTES TO POST we notice the track manager hustling down the corridor towards us. She's got on her long denim skirt and her runners with the flapping heel, some problem with the rubber—flap, flap.

"Here comes Daffy Duck," Mimi says, from one side of me.

Loo, on the other side, grunts.

We're hunched on stools in front of our terminals; twelve races into twenty-three—the day shift. We brace and wait for Patsy.

"You girls been using too much tape to pin up the race summaries," she shouts when she reaches us. "Half an inch is all you need. I been checking. Some of them summaries got two inch strips. Scotch Tape don't grow on trees, you know."

Loo's large Dutch face registers nothing. Mimi stares off.

I notice Patsy's hair, the way it's frizzed at the ends like a worn-out plastic broom, and think: This might be a detail I can use, later on.

When Patsy leaves Loo says, "Next time I spit on the summaries. Stick them up with my spit. Is so cheap here."

We get a laugh out of this. You'd think we were kids.

The PA comes on and it's Patsy with her prerecorded message. "Remember everyone. At Claymore Downs there are no late bets. Get your bets in early."

Her voice echoes throughout this dump of a place—concrete walls, no heat—a former racetrack turned simulcast. The concession stands are boarded up, the fences are half-standing, the racing turf is covered in weeds.

Live racing at Claymore Downs with crowds numbering in the thousands is a thing of the past. Now it's three middle-aged women—huddled at one end of a line that once saw dozens taking bets—serving the same forty or fifty gamblers. They roam the concourse like shades from the underworld: edgy, badly dressed, mostly men.

Bets are placed at our terminals via computer hookups to L.A., Toronto, Vancouver, Hong Kong. A bank of TV sets mounted high on the wall opposite where we sit shows the odds, and then the races. The gamblers stand before the screens, shielding their racing forms and their calculations from those nearby. If they win, they keep it to themselves; gambling is a greedy, secretive sport.

To those on the line, though, the change in the gamblers when they win is obvious; no longer the losers, the hard luck cases, they're brilliant handicappers now, confident geniuses, puffed-up and strutting.

"Remember, place your bets early," Patsy's message-voice blares. "Any wins over two thousand dollars must report to the office."

"I was always in the office," Mimi says. "At school. For smoking dope in the parking lot. Forging notes to get out of PE. Oh, I was bad." She likes the idea of being bad and laughs. She's a one-hundred-and-eighty-pound blonde who would still like to be bad but has a daughter in college. "Cramps my style," she says.

Ten minutes to post.

We know most of the gamblers by name: Larry the Loser; old Henry pushing a walker; Jack with his aged poodle tied up outside; Mel whose hands shake, who stinks of booze; the kid Jason who's on disability; Mean Mary who tips in nickels, if at all; Mary's sour husband Al; all the drunks who are sometimes barred from betting; the sly pensioners blowing their pension cheques; the guy with the bulbous nose who owns a clothing store in town.

Fred comes up to me with his usual two-dollar bet—a one four exacta box. I punch it in before he lays down his money.

"Thanks, Lucky." He takes the ticket.

Fred leaks woe. He's a baggage handler at the airport and has arthritis. His face is grey, and so is his uniform. He tells me the new pills are doing "diddly-squat."

"Poor Fred," Loo says. "With his measly two-dollar bets."

"It paid off last spring," I tell her. "That seven-hundred-dollar win. Bought new tires for his truck. That's why he comes to me. I'm his lucky charm."

"Poor bugger," Mimi says. "New tires? What's that?"

Mimi's wearing her white cowboy hat. Customers call her "The Hat." They call Loo "The Windmill" or "Tulip" because she was born in Holland and speaks with an accent. Fred's the only customer who calls me "Lucky;" otherwise I'm "The Professor." This is because I read between races. Today it's Agatha Christie, *Death on the Nile*—a young, beautiful, rich woman from England gets murdered while on holiday in Egypt. It's 1934. People have servants, change their clothes six times a day; say things to each other like, "I've just been touring the world." "How was the world?" "Gay, very gay."

"Do you think Ted will be in?" Mimi asks, scanning the crowd for her new regular, the guy who bets from a roll of fifties. Placing his bets, he stands sideways at her terminal and winks at her.

"Why don't he ask you out?" Loo says. "That kind of money."

"You think?"

"Paaah."

It's a Tuesday afternoon in late January, raining, cold inside. Patsy's left the Christmas decorations up; she says the customers like them.

Describing the scene later to my husband I say, "There's a green plastic tree with winking red lights in the corner beneath the TV sets."

He snorts. "God, that's depressing. Bring on the cellos from Eastern Europe." Then adds, "Write that down."

On the line we've got the tiny heater plugged into the wall behind us and take turns moving it around. Every three races one of us gets a hot back. The pay's a dollar above minimum, but there's tips—leftover change, sometimes more. Because of the tips we smile at the customers. Once I got a hundred-dollar bill that turned me into a Pavlovian dog and caused me to hope for the future.

Like the gamblers at Claymore Downs, I'm hooked on hope. For the big win—the big event—the singular breakthrough that will change my life. This is 1994 and I'm trying to be a serious writer. I call a story of mine "Drought on the Cash Flow River," but it's really an apology to my husband:

What I'm doing in this room will not make us rich. Sorry about that.

That story is truer than fiction: *I'm enslaved to a vagrant art that rewards fine sentences with a nod of recognition only. There really is a gun to my head. I put it there myself.*

He reads the story and says, "Huh."

Please don't pull the trigger.

Meanwhile I work at the track where my cash flow depends upon Patsy. Like many low-wage workers I'm at the mercy of a crank. Depending on her mood, and how well we avoid her wrath, we work four or five shifts a week. Friday and Saturday nights are best—more people, better tips. Those nights are owned by Marge, the weekend supervisor. A shrewd old woman of few words, Marge also collects the Old Age Security pension; she drives to work in a 1991 Lincoln. This is an interesting fact when compared to the cars most of the gamblers drive. They park their beaters on the cracked cement where the hamburger stands used to be. A lot of the gamblers don't own cars; a few, I know, walk to the track, and live in basement rooms. This is because any money they get goes on the horses. Off hours, I often see Larry walking home carrying plastic bags filled with groceries, or Dillon with a case of beer shoved under his arm.

Old Henry once told me that racetrack betting is an old man's sport, that it's too slow for the young—there's the calculations, the wait between races, the fact that it's all over in a couple of minutes. Judging by Claymore's customers, he's right; with the exception of Jason who's got a head injury, they're mostly old.

We have a run of betting until the post for Florida. A customer asks if I've cut my hair. Another bitches about the weather. I sell several hundred dollars worth of bets. When the race is over there'll be a few payouts, maybe tips—our little bit of heaven here behind the terminals.

Just before race sixteen at the Delmar track in L.A., heavy rain shuts down the computers. Customers hang around the TV sets grumbling.

Marty, a skinny guy in a baseball cap approaches my terminal. "This is bullshit," he says. "Call this a track? This place is a dump. This place is *beyond* a dump. Is anyone fixing things?"

"Dunno," I tell him. "Ask Patsy."

"Screw Patsy. Don't make me laugh."

I shrug—professionally—and catch sight of Willie the janitor hurrying by with his broom. Besides sweeping up losing tickets he's in charge of electrical outlets. Maybe a plug has fallen out of a socket. Who cares? I buy a roll of quarters from Mimi. I suck on one of Loo's fruit candies.

Waiting for our terminals to reboot, she reads an old *People* magazine. I carry on with Agatha Christie.

Mimi blows her nose. "My life is crap," she suddenly says. "Pure, unadulterated crap."

Loo looks up. "Count your blessings. Try having the sleeping sickness. That's what I got. *That's* crap."

We've just heard that Mimi's regular, Ted, is in Maui with his girlfriend. Mean Mary announces this after the last race when she leaves Mimi a forty-five-cent tip.

Then the terminals and the TVs flick on and we're back in business.

"Willie must've shoved his broom up one of them computers," Loo says. "You know, where the sun it does not shine."

"Ha. Ha." Mimi says, bored, and reprograms her machine.

This event releases Rose—Our Lady of the Permanent Scowl—from the cage beside the office where she counts the money. To do this she wears a visor like the bookies in the black and white movies.

We work off a four-hundred-dollar-float. When we take in a thousand over that, we bundle it up, fill out a form, and give it to Rose. She's very short, about four foot eleven, maybe sixty years old. On her days off she visits a tanning salon, the result being that her face looks like one of those touring mummies—shrunken and brown.

She takes my skim and growls, "Thank you, darling, sweetie, my love."

She makes a bet with Loo. "Give me a place on the two. Hurry up. Don't let anyone see you. Thank you, sweetie, my love, my darling."

We've given up trying to figure out Rose. The run of endearments coming from one so committedly foul no longer surprises us. Maybe she's got reverse Tourette's. Maybe "sweetie, darling, my love" are swear words to Rose.

"She and Patsy are some pair," Mimi says.

Strange, but I like being called "darling" by Rose; maybe I'm hard up for endearments.

WAITING FOR RACE NINETEEN to run in Vancouver, Loo starts talking: "You hear me ask Marge? Why didn't you pick me up? You hear what she say? Oh, I thought it was only one week. If she doesn't want to give me a ride she should say. Be direct. Is not right. I had to get my husband to bring me. Maybe I have to quit. I can't drive. I have the sleeping sickness. Last time I drove I woke up one inch from a telephone pole. That was too scary. Now I don't drive. Last summer I fell out of our apple tree. I never know when it will happen. I broke my arm. Now I can't climb apple trees. You hear me ask Patsy why she changed my machine? You see the way she hesitated?

Her eyes went glittery. She was lying when she said she didn't know anything about it. She knows. I'm being punished for being late. Because Marge didn't pick me up. Is not right. Why can't people be direct? Now I have a terrible machine. The tickets stick. Is so cheap here. No one fixes the machines. Yesterday I was short thirteen dollars. The machine repeats bets. How can you balance with a machine like that? Can we refuse to serve someone? That Spanish guy? He's so mean. When he comes to me I take my time. He always comes at post seconds before the race then gets pesky if I don't punch in his bets before the bell. So I pretend I don't understand him and he misses the race. Then he's really mad. But I don't care. I'm happy he's mad. Mr. Miserable. That man over there? Last race I paid him out. One hundred sixteen dollars. He gave me nothing. Is not right. They win and give you nothing. I'm working for peanuts."

I CLOSE OUT THIS DAY with twenty-three dollars worth of extra peanuts—my tips. I decide to use the money for gas, for a drive with my husband to China Beach, fifty miles past Victoria.

Afterwards I'll write a story in which we leave the track and the kids behind, in which we pack a lunch for the long drive, and toss warm jackets into the trunk of the car. Heading out the sun will be shining and we'll be grooving like the old days, weariness and want sliding off our backs like an Otis Redding song.

CONDOM RUN

I STOPPED IN at the birth control clinic. I was making a "condom run," as my husband calls it. The waiting room was filled with sweaty, sullen girls reading *People* and *Vogue* magazines and chewing on the orange and black jujubes that are left in a plastic bowl on the reception counter.

Staff at the birth control clinic have tried to make it a cheerful place. In the waiting area there are two colonial-style chesterfields draped with knitted afghans. Several stuffed animals sit on a wooden rocking chair. And the walls are painted a sunny yellow and decorated with bright posters about the symptoms of sexually transmitted diseases, the importance of using condoms. One poster has a provocative title: 100 Ways to Make Love without Having Sex. I had a closer look—it took some determined reading because the print was so small—but the list included going for beach walks at midnight and having long talks about "life."

The women who work at the birth control clinic are all

middle-aged or older, and every one of them is exuberantly friendly—an odd personality contrast to their clients, who are close-mouthed, even hostile.

The girls in the waiting room usually give me a sour look when I drop in, but I'm not deterred by their scorn because I'm on a mission. I'm hoping that the three young people who call our basement "home" will eventually consider personal responsibility as a life option. In the meantime, there's someone looking out for them.

Consumed with purpose, I fill my bag from the bowls of foil-covered condoms that are placed here and there about the room like appetizers at a party.

"Take as many as you like!" the woman behind the desk gaily tells me. And I realize that this woman and I are of one mind—zealots and pragmatists alike when it comes to the health and safety of our children.

I stuff perhaps fifty condoms into my purse, calculating with difficulty how many condoms per young person per week will be needed. This is difficult because when it comes to the sex lives of our children I can only guess what's going on. It's one of those taxing concepts, like trying to imagine the end of the universe. The mind stretches and it hurts.

IT'S MY CUSTOM to do a condom run every month or so. I add it to my list of things to do on a particular Friday afternoon. I'm rigid in my shopping habits: Friday is the only day I'll take myself away from things literary to do the grocery shopping. If we run out of frozen juice or cream cheese and bagels before then, I'm deaf to criticism. The cries of "There's nothing to eat!" that I routinely hear by Wednesday and Thursday have no effect on me. I tell everyone virtuously, "If all the juice is gone, drink water." And so on.

It shouldn't be surprising, then, that there's a crowd on hand Friday afternoons waiting for my return from the grocery store. And not only our kids...their friends, too. Word has gotten out. The feeling in the air is celebratory, like it is on Christmas or birthdays. And all because there are eight to ten bags of groceries in the trunk of my car.

"Did you get any orange cheese?" our twenty-year-old son Bill asks while unloading the car. There's a high degree of anxiety in his voice. He pays room and board now, so feels entitled to question my purchases. Only last week he left an angry note for me on the kitchen counter: "DO NOT JUST BUY ONLY LEMONADE!!!"

This is the son who announced, when he turned nineteen, that he was moving out to live with his rock band. My husband immediately went and bought a bottle of expensive French wine to celebrate. "Never in my wildest dreams did I think he'd move out so *soon*." He sounded positively giddy uncorking the wine. "I thought we'd have him *forever!*"

As moving day approached, Terry and I visited the paint store, spending an exhilarating ten seconds choosing the first cream colour we saw on the paint palette. Our plan was to repaint Bill's bedroom.

"You know," Terry said, driving home from the paint store, "we haven't seen his walls for years! All those upside-down posters. Why did he put them like that, anyway? And think of the garbage we'll get to throw out!"

He spent the rest of the day happily looking around the house and the yard for the paint tray.

As moving day neared, Nana bought Bill a set of dishes for his "new place." We made a special trip to Zellers and spent the morning consulting with one another over dish styles. "It's important to have good things," Nana declared, finally choosing an earthenware "starter" set, white with blue trim.

The "new place" was a rundown shack in Sidney. It was going to be the home of three of the four members of Bill's band. The band's name, I CAN'T STAND YOU, was scrawled on the outside front wall in large black letters. Inside the house: a vast collection of beer cans; two broken chesterfields; a grey Arborite kitchen table and two chairs; a bathroom with a broken shower; two tiny bedrooms and three single mattresses; a set of drums and three very large amps.

"We can save money by using the place for jamming," Bill told us, indicating that he at least understood the principles of personal budgeting. "Now we won't have to rent a separate jamming spot."

He was, it appeared, unconcerned about the fact that the police station was a block down the road.

"Won't be a problem," he explained when I pointed out things like noise and late-night parties. "All the neighbours are really old and take sleeping pills so they won't even be awake to complain to the cops." He named the new place "The Shack."

THE DAY BEFORE THE MOVE, I took Bill grocery shopping.

"To start him off," I told Terry. He looked at me dubiously.

That night we had a send-off dinner where Nana tearfully remembered every family member who had ever left home. "I just cried and cried watching them go out the door," she said, repeatedly. "To think of them so young and alone in the world."

"He's only ten minutes away, for god's sake!" Terry said.

"Yeah," Bill said, shoving the celebratory barbecued steak into his mouth. "I'll come visit now and then. You can make me tea."

Anna said, "Can I use his room as a den? You know, put in a chesterfield and TV and have parties in there?"

We told her no, it would be a guest room. Just saying "guest room" made me feel exalted; we'd never had such a thing before.

I cried on moving day. "So young and alone," I kept thinking.

At noon Terry called from work. "Has he gone yet?"

"He's still in bed."

"For Christ's sake!"

I went downstairs to Bill's bedroom. He was asleep in a nest of quilts and pillows. His cat, Bob, was lying on his back purring. The walls were bare, the shelves gutted. A cardboard box beside the bed was filled with clothes.

"Shouldn't you be leaving?"

Bill came awake, mumbling from beneath a pillow, "Yeah, later."

I gazed fondly at our firstborn. A young man with focus, with a determined set of "life goals." After a year of university he'd decided to work in a restaurant and devote his life to the band. When this decision was announced, Terry, who was certain our son would become a professional soccer player, or at the very least, a high school PE teacher, said to me, "Congratulations, Marion! We've just given the world another dishwasher."

BUT BILL EVENTUALLY MOVED OUT. It took the rest of the day. The actual moving out part—loading his belongings into his car—took maybe ten minutes. The rest of the time was spent drinking tea, using our CD player "one last time," playing with his cat (who wasn't accompanying him), washing his sizable collection of polyester slacks from Value Village, the ones he buys in the extra-large size then flamboyantly cinches to his six-foot, 142-pound body.

As for cleaning out his room, I was relieved to see he'd

taken the two hundred packs of condoms I'd left on his bed-side table. I'd made a special "run" for them.

"Two hundred condoms? A bit excessive, don't you think?" Terry said.

"Well..." I sniffed. "Well...."

The next day my husband painted the empty bedroom. "Leave me alone," he told me when I offered to help. "I want to do it myself. I'm anticipating a peak experience."

THE FIRST WEEKEND after our son's move we had a house guest, a young poet from Vancouver who was in town to give a reading. The new guest room looked beautiful: cream walls, vacuumed rug, a window you could actually see through, a single bed covered with a white Hudson's Bay blanket. Even the poet appreciated the room. When we took her down there she said, "A good place to do some reading," and flung her pack on the bed.

The next morning we found her asleep on the upstairs chesterfield. This was startling because the chesterfield is right outside our bedroom. It's the place our kids always go to when they're sick—a holdover from their younger days, a gesture of being closer to us in time of need. I thought maybe the poet had had a nightmare. Or was frightened sleeping alone in the downstairs room. Being from the city maybe she was spooked by so much silence. Or maybe she was sick.

Controlling my need to feel her forehead, I let her sleep. We tiptoed around her for much of the morning. She looked sweet laying there, her face pink and sweaty. Like one of our kids, really. She'd carted a pillow and the Hudson's Bay blanket upstairs with her. Her sock feet hung over the end of the chesterfield.

The dog's barking woke her at 11:30.

"Are you all right?" I asked.

Yes, she was fine, she told us crankily, now that she'd had some sleep. It was the girls in their room next door keeping her awake. Sneaking in their bedroom window at midnight, they'd carried on laughing and watching TV until 4 in the morning.

We apologized, gave the poet breakfast, and took her to the ferry.

When we got back, Bill's battered red Maverick was in the driveway. We found him in bed in the guest room.

"I've got a sore throat," he groaned. "And there's nothing to eat at The Shack. Can you make me some tea?"

I had a talk with Anna and Kristy. "That was very inconsiderate of you, keeping our guest awake like that. How many times have I told you there's no need to climb in the bedroom window? You can walk through the mud-room door like normal, grown-up people. Only fourteen-year-old babies climb through windows. You're both well past that now. This is what you do: You take off your shoes and tiptoe quietly down the stairs to your room. It's an age-old tradition."

TEN DAYS LATER Bill moved back home. "Do you even *know* how expensive it is out there?" he asked, accusingly, citing as evidence an "unreal" phone bill and the fact that "all of Sidney" was eating out of their fridge. He'd been gone for eighteen days in total.

"Eighteen days of bliss," Terry sighed, watching him unload his car.

"He obviously wasn't ready," I said.

"Uncle Rickey moved in and out at least a dozen times before he left home for good when he was thirty-seven," Nana said happily. She was standing with us on the front porch.

Our son grinned at the three of us as he struggled past with his TV set. He didn't seem at all embarrassed about returning home so soon.

After everything was back in his room, Nana invited all of us to her downstairs suite for tea. While Bill munched contentedly on the cookies his grandmother had made in advance for this occasion, my husband whispered to me: "One move down, eleven to go."

Later, after poking his head into Bill's room, he announced, "The posters are back on the walls. Right way up this time. I guess that's something."

I went and had a look. Everything was as before, only cleaner. The box of dishes, unopened, was shoved in the closet. The TV was back on the dresser, the cat was asleep on the bed. Only the condoms weren't in evidence. I'd had in mind sneakily counting how many of the two hundred were left. In this way, my condom calculations might be more accurate.

"Um," I said, interrupting Bill watching *Soccer Saturday*. "Um...where are all the condoms I left?"

"The girls took them," he said. "They've been selling them at school. Didn't you know? They were choked about not having condom machines in the washrooms. It's some protest thing they're having about student rights. They've made signs. You'll probably be getting a call about it next week from the school...."

THE PRINCESS, THE QUEEN, & THE WITHERED KING

THERE'S A PLACE CALLED Wit's End and I live there. It's a black place filled with guilt and accusation, practically a storybook place. A place where evil queen mothers dwell, disguised as hump-backed, hand-wringing crones. Supremely ugly, eternally disgusting. Every princess knows to avoid them, has been trained from birth to revile them, these victims of makeovers in reverse, these controlling, fun-sapping mothers. Nightly we crawl into our miserable holes, lick our festering wounds, and prepare for the next day's battle.

THE BATTLEFIELD AWAITS. *It's the breakfast table and the queen is screaming: "You've got two minutes before your ride leaves for school!!!" Spit flying, eyes bulging.*

The princess is serene, applying mascara before a compact mirror, her cereal uneaten. "Calm down," she growls.

Already the king is in the car honking the horn. There's a king? Yes, my god, poor thing, a hairless, skinny king, reduced to muteness, reduced to tossing his eyes at the ceiling. His eyes, these days, regularly exploding out of his head like champagne corks. The ceiling bruised, a moonscape. He's in the car now, backing it up, grimly asserting what's left of his kingness. The queen hears the threatening crunch of tire on gravel. Oh no! Her lips purse into a million wrinkles (so ugly!), her heart is racing (such uselessness), her hands are damp (wet claws). "All right," she snaps, "miss your ride, be late for school... f-f-f-fail English...." Snapping like a half-mad terrier. Snap, snap.

The princess, still unconcerned, saunters out the door barefoot, boots in hand, stopping before the kitchen window to have a last look at her lovely self, then wanders up the drive to the retreating car. The pathetic queen on the front porch calling, "Say goodbye!" The princess deigning to speak without turning her head: "Yeah, whatever."

THE FACE OF A MOTHER in battle is not pretty: red eyes, blotchy skin, the lines around the mouth etched in grimness. The daughter, on the other hand, is radiant—haughty, aloof, flushed with health, adept at tossing her head in pity and disdain.

Here at Wit's End her father and I huddle, snatch anxious consultations in the bathroom, whisper over the supper table. Eye contact, imperceptible nods become an art form of understated communication. The battles are fast-paced, the maneuvering tricky. Unpredictable mortar attacks from unpredictable demands can occur at any moment. ("Can I have that peach cooler in the fridge for breakfast?" "I'm moving to Arizona to be a waitress. So what if I'm fourteen.") Everything is liable to happen. To not happen.

Morning storms are the worst, when her mood is not even civil, when demands are the strongest, responses nasty. *Nasty.* A word that's suddenly on our lips, hauled from the depths. A word in waiting. Amazing how it fits everything. "That was a *nasty* look." "I don't like the *nasty* tone of your voice." "Why must you be so *NASTY?*" From the Dutch word *nestig* meaning dirty. Yes, the fighting is dirty, sly.

THE QUEEN'S NOSE *is twitching. The princess has just returned to the castle and floated through the living room where the queen is lying on the couch reading* How to Deal With Your Acting Up Teenager. *There's a certain smell...*

Today the princess's hair is a shade of orange; she's wearing the king's Christmas boxer shorts—red Santas on a green background—hiking boots and a yellow nylon jacket, never seen before, the kind, the queen believes, maniacs wear.

The queen's nose is twitching but she's about to use a new strategy, throw the princess off guard. She is going to use the word "darling." As well, following the book's advice, she is going to appear as languid and lovely as her daughter. (But there's that smell...)

"Hello, darling," the queen says, her breath, studied, dreamy. "Where did you get the jacket?"

"Wha?" the princess says, momentarily arrested. "Who?..."

Once upon a time, long, long ago, the queen got stoned. Many, many times. So many times, in fact, that this present, certain smell takes her back. But not to fourteen. At fourteen the queen remembers going to movies, having pyjama parties, curling her girlfriend's hair, giggling about boys. Her mind wasn't twisted, blown, or dulled until she was well on in age—nineteen, twenty-one.

*The queen is being cunning, hoping she sounds bored.
"Darling," she asks. "What's that smell on you?"*

*A brief look of panic disturbs the princess's lovely
countenance, her glassy eyes focus, stare down at the
strangely relaxed queen.*

*The princess says, "I hate it when you're like this. You're
so...so...different."*

*The queen smiles at her daughter's retreating back.
Satisfaction. Score one for the queen. Now if only she could
maintain this course... What does the book say?*

THE BOOK SAYS: "Give them responsibility for their own lives;"
"Stand up for yourself;" "Assert your rights;" "Steal center
stage;" "Don't be sucked into giving them negative attention."

Alright, alright! But at times our daughter's brainpower
is staggering and we have to always be on the alert, scanning
the skies for incoming missiles. There's the ability she has to
set us up, push the right (wrong!) buttons. There's her subtle
manipulations, the way she can lie so sweetly, sound so reasonable. Ah ha! A foil! we cry. We know *that* one, we've
done it ourselves; we know how easy it is to lie. Heartless we
were, just like she is, and conniving. Wouldn't I always try to
get my way? Do anything, say anything to go to the party,
date the wrong boy? And the king! The withered king who
these days can't even get the dog to obey. At sixteen he had
a spare set of keys made for his mother's car. The sneaky future
king stealing his mother's car, roaring around town in the
small hours, drunk and belligerent.

THREE A.M. IN THE CASTLE. *Sleepless again, the queen is at her desk
composing a MANIFESTO, thinking, "Perhaps the light*

approach." Next day the princess reads the MANIFESTO stuck to the fridge door:

1. We are firm but reasonable parents; we don't scream (hardly ever) or hit; we simply lay down the rules. Consequences occur if rules are broken.

2. We are open to negotiation. We are not deaf; we are as flexible as grass in the wind.

3. Generally we are loving and kind. Specifically, we encounter periodic emotional disturbance with skill, patience, and every street fighting tactic we can remember.

4. Moment to moment resolutions mean nothing, although we cannot ignore the moments. Nevertheless, we will not anticipate bad moments; bad moments will not exist until they are hurled upon us. We will live our happy fulfilled lives, thinking greater thoughts, having calm, enriching emotions, having a multitude of good moments. Breathing deeply. Counting to ten.

5. We will consume alcohol as required: a glass or two of sherry during skirmishes has proven helpful. A bottle of wine per weekend night is de rigueur.

6. Presents and money will be showered upon said young person in adherence to ancient Pavlovian principles: You slobber on cue, you get the treat.

7. Our guiding words will be "big picture; intergalactic scheme of things; when we're a hundred." Hah! When you're *a hundred!*

8. We will make every effort to curb our pathological need to utter the words, "No, goddammit!"

THE PRINCESS TOSSES her shining blue hair. "Get a life," she says (would that be scorn in her voice?) "You guys are so pathetic. You think you know what's going on, but you don't."

What's going on? Booze? Drugs? Truancy? Partying at all costs? Hanging out? Scraping through school? Unprotected sex? Or none of this? Just going to movies? Having pyjama parties? Curling her girlfriend's hair? Giggling about boys?

THE QUEEN IS LONGING *for a bucket of sand in which to stick her head.*

When it is said disparagingly of other queens and kings: "Oh, they don't know what's going on," the queen thinks, "How wonderful! Not to know what's going on. I'd give anything for a few years of ignorance. I'd give my queendom. I'd give away my keys to the castle if only there was a suitable prince."

Would she? Never. There's isn't a suitable prince; so far they're all deadbeat teenage alcoholics whose descriptive vocabularies don't extend beyond the word "fuckin."

Nevertheless, the princess is howling, (her hair, this time, an arresting shade of Kool-Aid green), "What's the matter with Hayden? Just because he got kicked out of school, just because he's up on drug charges."

PEOPLE HAVE STOPPED ME on the street, pulled me aside at the grocery store to tell me how beautiful our daughter is: "She should be a model," they say. "She's gorgeous, a knockout!" This from the ignorant mothers of sons. Or from the mothers of grown-up daughters. These mothers are grinning zombies now, irreversibly brain damaged; they've completely forgotten the battles, the bloodshed at the front door. Then there's the saddest group of all, the new mothers of baby girls, the ones with fear in their eyes; they look at your teenage daughter as if she were an apparition, the stuff of science fiction—a phenomenon, like leprosy, something that could never happen to them.

THE QUEEN SUSPECTS *she might be having a nightmare. She's standing hands out, palms up, before a smug assembly of monarchs. These queens, she knows, consider themselves successful; their princesses do volunteer work, make the honour roll, do math without a calculator, read novels on a Friday night, iron their jeans.*

The queen is trying to explain: "But my princess has an incredible mind, she's so fast and articulate. And funny! When she's in the mood she can really make us laugh; she's such a mimic. And don't forget her fashion sense; it's so...so...different. And she does love her family, I'm certain of it—the way she always comes home. Given enough time, she'll be wonderful. Right now she's wonderful-in-training."

As the queen speaks, her words flutter to the ground like pieces of paper, like snapshots. There's that picture of the princess taken during her black period—lips, hair, nails. Another of her at twelve "pretending" to smoke.

But the assembly of monarchs is angry; they're pelting the queen with family photo albums. "It won't do!" several of them are shouting.

The queen runs for cover. It's either that or being pelted to death by fond memories.

GROWING UP, how many times did I hear: "You think of no one but yourself"? I said it myself only yesterday like some condemned parrot, all teeth and spit. "You don't care if I'm injured (bruised rib from stuck door on family junker), all you want from me is to cut your hair."

Here at Wit's End I'm holding my side in pain. *Pain*! The martyred mother howling neglect, howling the eternal sub-text: "You don't love me. If you loved me, you wouldn't..." (pick anything.) The princess is right, it's so pathetic, reviling, this grasping for love. A set-up for rejection.

But what I want to tell her is this: "Remember when I was the best mother in the world? And you were so direct with your love, leaving me notes on my pillow, telling me, 'I want to be just like you'? You held yourself up like a mirror, copied everything I did—the way I wore my hair, the way I walked. Oh, I was your idol! And now I've fallen. And it's me who can't abide your departure. It's me, the wicked queen, who would put you to sleep, preserve your childhood sweet-ness forever."

THE KING AND QUEEN *have bought a new second-hand car. It's a sporty job with a sunroof, finely upholstered seats, doors that easily open, and a tape deck that really works. It's a warm spring evening and they're thinking about taking a spin.*

The princess, late for dinner again, has just returned home. She's trudging down the driveway, shoulders bent from carrying a back pack that must weigh sixty pounds, filled as it is with every item of clothing that she owns. She's wearing a grey sweatshirt, her head covered with the hood, but it looks as if her hair sticking out the top is purple in colour, the same colour, the queen notes, as the trailing petunias in the garden.

The king and queen are about to get in the car. Lately they've rediscovered one another, have been observed on a Friday evening dancing together in the kitchen. On several occasions now they've left notes on the dining room table that say: "Gone out for dinner. Love XO."

"*Your hair—that's a pretty shade of purple,*" *the queen says to the princess. "Where did you colour it?"*

The princess glowers. "In the park." Then, narrowing her eyes: "Where are you going?"

"Out for a spin," the king says. "Want to come?"

"...No." (Was there a hesitation?)

"There's leftover spaghetti in the fridge if you're hungry," the queen adds, smiling.

The king, who's looking like a UN peacekeeper in his blue beret, puts a John Lee Hooker tape in the tape deck and cranks up the volume. The queen backs up the car. In the rear-view mirror she can see the princess standing on the front porch staring. Overwhelmed with love for this rough-edged, beautiful girl, she sticks her hand out the sunroof and waves.

"Where to?" the queen hollers above "Mad Man Blues" and the king hollers back, grinning, "Anywhere. It doesn't matter. Who the hell cares?"

ANIMALS AT THE EMPRESS

MY HUSBAND COLLECTS HARDWARE. I collect towels, pulling them from my flesh like feathers.

"It's biology," my husband tells me. "We're mammals. You feather the nest. I protect it."

I admire his certainty, watching like Jane Goodall for tell-tale signs, the rampant hooting and chest pounding behaviour favoured by apes the world over. It's me in my trim khaki shorts hovering in the blind, peering at him, taking notes.

"Blind!" he shrieks when I tell him this, summing up my position on his Tarzan theory.

His latest purchases are displayed on the dining room table—a soldering gun and a glue gun. They remain virginal in their boxes.

"Guns," I say, dismissively. "The dominant male of this household is collecting guns."

"Of course!" he says, floored by my ignorance. "How else to protect the den?"

"A soldering gun and a glue gun are going to protect us? From what? Soldering and glue-wielding predators?"

"You never know," he says, happily stroking the boxes.

He's clearly pleased. Buying hardware gives him a rush, he says; their purchase comes with a tingle of glee, like a supplementary warranty. The new items are about to take their place in the basement alongside the jars of nails, the wrench sets, the unused skill saw—booty hoarded against a time of want.

In truth, it's the same for me with the towels, sheets, pillowcases, and dishcloths I've started collecting. I've developed an unseemly interest in thread count—the higher the count, the better. Sheets with a thread count of two hundred and eighty can send me soaring.

Collecting hardware and linen is a recent practice of ours. While the kids were growing up it seemed we had one grubby towel apiece. Now that they're older and threatening to leave home we're getting prepared for a time of plenty.

"Do you think it's sexual?" I ask my husband. "Collecting hardware and linen? Do you think it's some kind of weird, middle-aged aphrodisiac?"

"Could be," he says, suggesting a quickie visit to the flashing aisle at Slegg Lumber to test the theory.

"Is there something I'm missing?" I ask. "Like hardware and linen X-rated movies? Burly men, naked except for a carpenter's apron, meeting up with buxom saleswomen from linen departments?"

"Could be," he repeats, and then heads for the basement mumbling, "I know there's a carpenter's apron down here somewhere."

He passes our oldest, twenty-one-year-old Bill, on the stairs. "Where's Dad going in such a hurry?"

"Gone to gaze fondly at his tools."

"Huh?"

Moments later my husband returns from the basement but not with a carpenter's apron. He's clutching three brass numbers. "Look what I found!" he cries. "The door numbers from the Empress Hotel!"

Dusting them off he's beside himself. "Remember how I got these?" he laughs, polishing the recovered treasure on his sleeve.

"How?" Bill asks on cue, and the bait is set. We sit down.

"From when the Empress Hotel was being renovated, ten, twelve years ago," my husband says with amazement. "When I had that roofing business."

"When you had that *going-out-of-business* roofing business," I add.

"It was just before Christmas and things were tight," he says, ignoring my comment. "Me and some guys from the Sidney Hotel thought we'd haul away the old doors and make a bundle. Remember?"

"Of course I remember. Christmas dinner that year was going to be roast seagull and all the trimmings."

Bill glances at me, shocked. "You weren't seriously going to feed us seagull."

"Times were tough," I reply. "We had to make our own fun."

My husband begins his story. "I was in the Sidney Hotel. It was late afternoon, near Christmas, and I was nursing a beer, worrying about things. When Bobby Ryan shows up telling me he's got this deal to make some fast money but he needs some help. Ordinarily I'd avoid Bobby Ryan. He's not the sharpest knife in the drawer. But this deal didn't sound too bad. All he needed was two or three guys to help him load doors onto his truck. The Empress Hotel in Victoria was being renovated and there were all these heavy wooden doors stacked beside the hotel. Bobby knew the guy who was in on the wrecking and this guy said, 'Pick 'em up and they're yours.'"

"For free?" Bill asks.

"Yeah, for free. So we're sitting in the bar and there's this terrible storm outside. Rain's smashing against the windows. 'Jeez, you wanna go now,' I says, because it was so rotten out, and Bobby says, 'It's now or never. We'll split the doors between us,' he says, 'they're worth a bundle. We can sell them for two hundred bucks a door.'"

"I did some quick calculations. Five doors would be worth a thousand bucks. Twenty doors, four thousand. And wouldn't that kind of money come in handy, being Christmas and all? So we grab two other guys from the bar. Old Knobby, half-drunk, and Howard, a Native kid with nothing to do.

"The four of us squeeze into the cab of Bobby's truck—a Chev that's seen better days—and head down the highway to Victoria. Even though the rain's coming down sideways, even though the stoplights are swinging in the wind, we're having a hoot figuring out all the money we're gonna make.

"By the time we get to the front door of the Empress Hotel it's dark out and the rain and wind are even worse. There's a group of doormen in purple uniforms huddled together under the awning trying to stay dry and Bobby asks one of them where the old doors are stacked. The doormen don't know what we're talking about and thinking we're riff-raff tell us to move along. But on a hunch, Bobby drives to the back of the hotel, to the parking lot, and there they are, thrown on a burning pile, maybe a hundred doors, some still with the hardware on. The brass rings and numbers.

"So we get to work. Not as easy as it sounds. Each door weighs a ton and there's only Howard and me doing the grunt work. Knobby's useless. He's passed out in the truck, and Bobby says his back won't take the lifting. Plus he's being a pain in the ass, acting like a big shot foreman, telling us which doors to take and which ones to leave.

"We're loading the doors in the glare of the truck's headlights and the wind's so bad we can hardly stand. Behind us the Empress Hotel's looming up like some gigantic cruise ship. It's all lit up with these warm orange lights, and I keep thinking I'm in the wrong place. That I should be *inside* the hotel, in the Bengal room, sitting by the fire there, sipping a hot rum. Not out here in the storm slaving my ass off.

"After loading twenty doors I says to Bobby, That's it. Because that's all we can fit in the truck bed and I'm soaked through and freezing and want to go home. So we figure the split. Six doors each and two for Knobby just for coming along. Six doors could mean twelve hundred dollars.

"Driving out from Victoria to Sidney the truck's groaning. Not only from carrying the doors, but from four guys in the cab as well. We make it as far as the Waddling Dog Inn on the highway, three miles south of Sidney, when the rear shocks give out—wham! Fortunately the Waddling Dog Inn is right there, the idea being we'll go in for a beer and tomorrow we'll get another truck from someplace and unload the doors. Before we head off I pry three numbers from a door on top of the stack.

Bill and I look at the shiny numbers now sitting on the dining room table alongside the soldering gun and the glue gun. A 4, a 7, and an 8.

"What happened to the doors?" Bill asks, fingering the 8, his favourite number.

"The whole thing was a bust," my husband says, and laughs. "Inside the Waddling Dog Inn we talked it up big, hoping for some sales. Got these doors from the Empress Hotel! We told anyone who'd listen. Own a piece of history! Only two hundred bucks! And then it was—only one hundred bucks! Then—only fifty bucks! But nobody bought a door that night. And the next day Bobby couldn't find a truck. And I got a terrible cold from getting soaked—had to take a cab home—so stayed in bed. No one else did anything, either. Bobby's truck sat on the side of the road for a week, the doors getting rained on till they were warped and useless. Finally, Howard's cousins on the reserve hauled them away for firewood."

"Bummer," Bill declares.

My husband, the hunter-gatherer, sighs in agreement, and places the three numbers on the coffee table. They've become hallowed, a bright reminder of riches denied.

THE FOLLOWING DAY I find my husband sitting in the living room holding number 7 and rubbing it like a lucky charm. Bill stumbles into the kitchen; he's just got up and proudly tells me he's got a killer hangover.

Hearing this, my husband's eyes snap open. The animal in him has resurfaced and he strides into the kitchen bellowing. "Time for the dominant male to nudge the young buck off the savannah! Time for a talk about your Life Plan!"

Bill looks at him with a mixture of surprise and terror. "What do you mean?" he croaks, a skinny, six-foot-tall man rubbing his eyes like a toddler.

"A full-time job is what I mean," my husband roars. "For starters. Working part-time in a cappuccino bar is not a full-time job. When I was twenty-one I was working eighty hours a week at the steel mill."

"There's been some terrible mistake," Bill pleads. "I'm really only nineteen. All my friends are nineteen. That's the age I really am."

"When I was nineteen," my husband says, "I was working

two hundred hours a week in a men's clothing store. And still had time for hangovers!"

"I've got a headache," Bill groans.

"Everyone has a headache," my husband cries. "It's part of being an adult."

"But this headache is like a lightning bolt shooting through my skull," Bill insists.

My husband grins mercilessly. "The very one I'm talking about. I've had that headache for twenty-one years!"

"You're going to turn out just like Uncle Kenny," I wail.

"Here we go," Bill sighs.

"Uncle Kenny didn't leave home until his widowed mother died. He was sixty-one!"

"I'm not Uncle Kenny," Bill mumbles.

"Prove it!" my husband snorts, resting his case.

The proof came a couple of weeks later. Bill, together with Anna and Kristy, have pooled their money and reserved a room for us at the Empress Hotel.

"What for?" my husband asks suspiciously.

"For old time's sake," Bill says, winking at the girls. "And because we're responsible young adults giving their parents a one-night vacation."

Showing us the brochure, Bill reads, "You'll experience hospitality in the grand style that recalls the genteel days of brigadiers and business barons, dowagers, and debutantes."

The three of them grin at us like executioners.

"And if there's a party, all of you are out on the street," my husband yells the following weekend as we're getting in the car.

"Sure, sure," the kids laugh, closing the front door before we're even left the driveway.

"Do you think the kids suspect we'll be doing something other than fondling the enormous white towels in the bathroom or stroking the brass numbers on the door to our room?" I muse.

"I'm way ahead of you," my husband says. "After a couple of hot rums in the Bengal room, I'd planned on unpacking the new carpenter's apron I've bought just for tonight...."

"No!" I shriek.

"Yes!" You'll be the debutante in the white towel and I'll be the brigadier in the carpenter's apron. Then, afterwards, we'll hang out the sixth floor window and hoot like monkeys in the trees."

TIC-TAC-DOE

BECAUSE WE COULDN'T SELL our 1980 Peugeot—it had a blown head gasket—I phoned a number advertised in the community paper: *TIC-TAC-DOE CABINETS—Will trade kitchen cabinets for something of value.* I told the man on the line that what we wanted were bathroom cabinets and the area around the tub tiled. If he could do this we would give him the car.

"All it needs is a head gasket," I said. "And it's in beautiful shape. The body's great, a dark wine colour. It's got plush interior and a sunroof. It looks like a Mercedes."

He said he was interested and we arranged a time for him to come and look at the job.

"What's your name?" I asked.

"Tickner. Daryl Tickner."

TWO NIGHTS LATER Daryl Tickner drove up in a beige 1972 Plymouth with large patches of rust around the rear wheels. A man in his late thirties, tall but solidly built, wearing black cowboy boots. He had a long thin ponytail which hung over his plaid jacket. The jacket was dirty with smears of oil on the sleeves and chest. He wore a diamond stud in his left ear.

He took off his boots when he came in the house. Then looked at the bathroom. The sink area consisted of a platform of white melamine board, a curtain (green and yellow flowers) hung in place of cabinet drawers, and the floor was covered in lime green tiles, a colour that for some reason I had loved deeply in 1984. To complete the sordid effect, the sheeting around the bathtub was cracked and warped; black mould was growing around the edges.

Of this Daryl said, "It'll have to be replaced before we can put on tile. I'll have to rip it out and put up half-inch plywood first." He sounded disgusted.

He put his boots back on and went outside with my husband to look at the car. It had been sitting in the driveway for a year and a half and one of the rear tires was flat. Daryl opened a front door and peered inside the car. Then he looked under the hood. It was impossible to guess what he was thinking.

I watched the men from the vestibule window. They walked solemnly around the car several times, then leaned against the hood and had a smoke.

Then they came inside. This time Daryl left his boots on.

"Nothing else wrong with the car besides the head gasket?" he asked.

"No."

"All right," he said, "I'll do it but I'll need three hundred dollars for materials. I've got to get the cabinet top and the wood to build the cabinets. I'll trade my labour for the car.

You pick up the tile you want for the tub. Soon as we get that I'll have my partner out here laying her up."

He wanted the three hundred dollars up front. We balked.

"I can't be putting out money like that," he said, "what with a family to feed."

"A family to feed, yes, of course," we said anxiously. And agreed to his terms. How much longer would the car sit in the driveway unless we did? How much longer would the rot and mould around the bathtub continue to disgrace us?

Before we gave him the money, though, we wanted a reference.

"No problem," Daryl said. And gave us the name and phone number of a Dr. Donnelly. "I put in his kitchen. Call him tonight if you want."

It was a Monday night.

"You get the tile by the weekend and the cash to me tomorrow morning and we can sign the contract. The bathroom will be finished this time next week. But I don't work Sunday," he added. "I never work on the Lord's day."

AFTER DARYL LEFT I found the number of Dr. Donnelly in the phone book. He was listed at a clinic on the other side of town. His phone number was different from the one Daryl gave us— probably his home phone, I reasoned. My husband did the phoning. He was grinning when he finished the call. "Dr. Donnelly says Daryl doesn't have hemorrhoids. And he said he did the work okay, there weren't any problems."

"So there really is a Dr. Donnelly?"

"Must be. He's in the book."

"Good," I said. "I'm sure Daryl needs the work. And if he's hooked into a church...."

"That's the oldest con in the book," my husband said.

"Guys talking about the Lord. That's what sucks people in. Especially old people. They think it means reliable, honest, trustworthy. Pretty soon they're having their roofs redone or their houses painted when they don't need it. And then it's thousands of dollars later. All because of a line about the Lord. I knew a guy called Ray who did this all the time. With him it was septic tanks. Digging them up for nothing."

But we went ahead with the deal.

THE NEXT MORNING I drove the forty miles to Daryl's house. It was 10:30 when I got there. A shabby house, white with light blue trim, at the end of a cul-de-sac. Two rusted cars in the driveway. An old blue pickup truck parked outside on the road.

After several minutes a man answered the door. Late forties, skinny, in his undershirt, unshaven.

"Sorry, I was asleep. Didn't hear the bell."

He asked me in.

"Daryl's out back. I'll get him."

"This is my partner Ray," Daryl said, introducing me to the man when he came in. "Ray Tacowski—the 'Tac' of Tic-Tac-Doe." Tattoos of snakes on both of Ray's forearms. I noticed most of Daryl's bottom teeth were missing.

We sat at the kitchen table. Ray had disappeared. There were children's drawings tacked on the wall and more drawings and notices on the fridge door. On the kitchen counter were several boxes of breakfast cereal lined up neatly, a jar of instant coffee, a jar of Coffee-mate. Looking into the dining room I could see a china cabinet filled with crystal wine glasses, china plates, cups and saucers. The place looked reassuring, like an established household.

Everything was business-like. Daryl had a contract ready

for me to sign. With a clause that said the contract was void
if the work wasn't completed within thirty days.

He showed me plans for someone else's kitchen. "Doing
cabinets in exchange for a motorhome," he said. "But I'll do
your bathroom first."

I gave him six fifty-dollar bills. He gave me a receipt.

"I'll be out tomorrow to take measurements," he said.

"What time?"

"After supper."

Later I told my husband: "I met the 'Tac' of Tic-Tac-Doe
Cabinets. Ray Tacowski. Wonder if it's the same Ray you
knew?"

"Fat guy? Bald?"

"No. He's skinny, got hair. Brown and greasy."

"Doesn't sound like the same Ray."

"Looks like an alcoholic. Shakes when he walks."

"Figures. They're both probably on step one of a nineteen-
step recovery program."

"Could be," I said. "Which is why we've got to hang in
there. People on recovery programs need our support."

"Mmmm."

"Anyway, they've got the money now."

"You didn't give them cash did you?"

"That's what he wanted."

"Jesus."

"What difference would a cheque make now? We're
already committed. It'll be all right, you'll see. His house
didn't look fly-by-night. It looked like a place where people
lived."

"So what? You think crooks don't live in houses?"

"If you're so worried why'd you agree to the deal?"

"Because it's the only way we'll get rid of the car," my
husband said.

That night we drove into town. We spent two hundred dollars on five boxes of white tile, a fifty-pound sack of mortar, a tub of grout, and a new toilet seat.

My husband stacked the materials on the front porch.

WE SAW DARYL three days later, Friday night.

"Jeez, sorry about the last few days," he said. "My son's been sick. I couldn't go anywhere."

We said we understood.

He took the bathroom measurements.

"What colour countertop?" he asked.

"White."

"I'll have to order it. You wouldn't want pink, would you? I've got some real nice pink."

"No," we said, "we want white."

A week later I phoned Daryl.

"Where have you been?"

"Jeez, I should have phoned. I got the flu. I been so sick I couldn't get out of bed. It's really put me behind. Remember I told you about my son being sick? I got it from him. Last night I had a temperature of a hundred and three."

I said I understood. And hoped he'd get well.

Another week went by.

"I keep trying to go to work," Daryl said when I phoned again, "but this bug's really laid me out. I've had to cancel the motorhome deal. All I do is sleep. But I've ordered the counter top. Should be here next week."

When I told my husband he said, "Flu, my ass. He's stalling till the thirty days are up on the contract. Then the deal will fall through. He'll have the three hundred bucks and we'll have dick. And just try to get the money back from him then. I know these guys. This is the way they operate."

"I wonder if Dr. Donnelly is the "Doe" of Tic-Tac-Doe Cabinets?" I said. Picturing another guy like Daryl and Ray, the janitor maybe at Dr. Donnelly's office. With the name of Don. Hanging around waiting for the call from pigeons like us. Picturing the Three Stooges with a sinister twist.

I called Daryl twice the following week. The first time he told me the counter top had come in and that he'd been working on the cabinets. "But the damnedest thing happened today," he said, "a bearing on my saw broke. If I can't fix it I'll have to get a new saw."

The other call was 10 a.m. on a Saturday morning. A woman answered the phone. When I asked for Daryl she said, "He's in bed."

I started to tell her why I was calling: "It's about the cabinets.... I was wondering if he's bringing them out today."

"Just a minute," she said, sounding annoyed, and went and got him.

"Yeah, they're just about finished," Daryl said when he finally got on the line. "I'll bring them out on Monday and we can wrap the whole job up in two days."

It was eight days later, on a Sunday that we saw Daryl. After several more calls from me he said he could see I was getting antsy. "I don't usually work on the Lord's day," he said, "but for you I'll make an exception; I'll come out after church and we'll get started."

"What time will that be?"

"After lunch," he said. "But I don't have the cabinets together."

"Bring the countertop anyway," I said, thinking, at least we'll have something to show for our money.

At 3 he drove up.

"Sorry I'm late," he said. "But the damnedest thing happened. I was getting gas beside the Waddling Dog Inn and who should I bump into but my lawyer. So we went and had a beer. Haven't seen him in a coon's age."

The countertop was in the back seat of his car. White. It looked okay. He stopped when he was carrying it into the house to have a look at the tile on the front porch. "That's the tile, eh?" he said. And sighed.

Then he got to work tearing the bathroom apart. He pulled the sheeting away from the tub. "Look at that," he said, almost delighted. "You've got an ant's nest in there."

We put on the bathroom fan because the mildew smell was so bad. Moments later he asked me for a cold drink. Not long after this my husband asked me for a Band-Aid. He said Daryl had a rash on his hand that he wanted to cover.

The tearing apart, the sawing, the hauling drywall outside continued for an hour. I was making supper. My husband was helping Daryl. Before long he came into the kitchen and said Daryl was sitting on the edge of the bathtub holding his jaw. "He's got a toothache."

Minutes later I met Daryl in the hallway. He looked miserable. His hand was still holding his jaw. "It's killing me," he said, "I've got to go."

I said I understood.

After he'd gone my husband said, "At least he's left his tools. He'll have to come back and finish the job now."

We looked at the tools: a wooden tool box, a battery driven drill, a hand saw, tape measures, a level, and three new hammers with the price tags still on—all $49.95.

"He probably bought those with our three hundred dollars," my husband said.

He'd left his jacket, too, thrown on the bathroom floor.

The only problem was that now the bathroom was completely useless. Daryl had disconnected the bolts to the toilet and the bathtub was filled with mouldy debris from the walls. The pink insulation on the walls was exposed and the bathroom floor was splattered with used drywall mud. This meant we had to use the toilet in the basement.

"We paid three hundred dollars for some guy to come and trash our bathroom," my husband said.

I left the sheets on the floor covering the route from the front door to the bathroom. Because I was certain we'd see Daryl tomorrow.

I should have known better: the toothache. He'd seen his dentist, he was on antibiotics, he'd had to stop four times on the drive home from our place because of the pain; the pain was so bad he could hardly see, he'd had a temperature of a hundred and three.

"What? A hundred and three again?" my husband said.

"So maybe he's sickly," I said. "But he's trying. You can tell he's trying. He says he'll be out tomorrow for sure."

At 8:15 the next morning Daryl phoned: "I'll be out later this morning. I'm just finishing up the cabinets."

When my husband phoned from work to see if Daryl had shown up I told him about the early call. "8:15 in the morning," I said, impressed.

"Up at 8:15?" my husband said. "He must have shit the bed."

At 3:30 I phoned Daryl.

"What happened?"

"You won't believe my day." he said. "But I won't bore you with the details. We'll get it done tomorrow. That's a promise."

THAT NIGHT MY HUSBAND SAID: "I'm going to phone him up, tell him to keep the three hundred dollars and I'll keep his tools. And I'll finish the goddamned bathroom myself."

I managed to calm him down. "Confrontation won't get us anywhere," I said. "And who's going to buy a bunch of tools, most of which are used? The only way we're going to get those cabinets is by playing along with him, waiting it out. We already have the countertop and we haven't signed over the car yet. If we just hang in there a little longer, I'm sure it will work out. He's obviously learning how to be reliable."

"This is just like social work," said my husband, who works with the behaviour problems at the local middle school.

Meanwhile there was the mildew smell coming from the bathroom. And the 3 a.m. treks downstairs in the dark to pee.

Two days later Daryl and Ray showed up with the cabinets. It was the first time Ray had been to the house. The delay in their arrival was because they'd had to borrow a truck. ("My brother's got my Aerostar.") It was 6:30. I'd phoned their place at 5. A kid had answered the phone. "No he's not here, he'll be back in an hour."

"Is he delivering cabinets?" I asked, hoping I didn't sound too desperate.

"Just a minute," the kid said. I heard a woman's voice in the background, and then the kid told me uncertainly, "Yeah, he's delivering cabinets." I pictured Daryl sitting at his kitchen table and mouthing to the kid: *Tell her I'm not home.* And eating his supper of canned spaghetti and beer and laughing.

SO I WAS HAPPY AND RELIEVED when they actually showed up. They carried the cabinet frames into the house, puffing and laughing. Ray was wearing a T-shirt that said "Crazy Gringo."

"No doors or drawers yet," Daryl said happily. "But they're just about finished." They'd brought two sheets of plywood, as well, for nailing up around the tub, and left them propped against the house. They were in a good mood, pleasant, talkative. Proud of themselves, it seemed, for actually delivering the goods.

They stayed long enough to bring the cabinets into the hallway and tell us they'd be back tomorrow. Which, miraculously, they were, managing to work three straight hours and arriving only four hours later than they said. This day was their most productive; they nailed up the plywood and got the cabinets in place. I made them coffee, telling them I'd be back in fifteen minutes, I had to pick up my son from school. When we returned they were sitting inside the Peugeot. Daryl was in the driver's seat, his hands on the steering wheel. It looked like they were pretending they were driving somewhere.

After that the pace picked up. Slightly. We got two more two-hour work days out of them. When Daryl said they'd be out midmorning, I blithely told my husband that it would be mid-afternoon. And it was. Unloading the cabinet doors from his car trunk Daryl said, "I've nearly had a nervous breakdown doing this job." And I said, "So have we!"

During these days Daryl and Ray laughed together while they worked. And they had long conversations about the right way to hammer in the cabinets and even one about a woman who wore Coke-bottle glasses: "You could dump a pot of potatoes over her head and she wouldn't know." Ray said. "Jeez, it'd blow my mind if I couldn't see." Daryl sang hymns while he worked: "Rock of Ages" and "Onward Christian Soldiers."

The toilet had been removed by now and sat on blocks on the front porch like an old car that would one day be worked on—our toilet rudely exposed for the neighbours to see: its shocking white body, its sad, empty bowl. I recited to my husband the first lines of a poem by Russell Edson: "The toilet slides into the living room on its track of slime demanding to be loved...."

I found myself happy to see Daryl and Ray when they'd finally arrive for their daily two hours. The bathroom was getting worked on, something was happening. Ray turned out to be a talker; he told me to get rid of the English ivy in our yard because it was killing the pear tree. He said he'd been in the tree business for fifteen years (removing trees that didn't need removing?) and said he knew what he was talking about. When Ray wasn't telling me about his past businesses (trees, roofs, windows), sawing bits of plywood, or cutting tiles, he was rolling cigarettes, playing tag with the dog or using the bathroom downstairs. He was polite but very nervous. I noticed that when he sat on the front porch smoking he couldn't keep his legs still; they shook of their own accord. But the work progressed. Daryl seemed quite moved and said thank you when I told him that the job was looking good.

But this pair of two-hour work days turned out to be our Golden Age with Tic-Tac-Doe Cabinets. It's true Daryl and Ray finally got the tile on the walls, but it was clear they didn't know what they were doing. The tiles were placed crookedly, mortar was splattered on the ceiling, the bathtub, the floor. And many of the tiles were chipped. Neither of them knew about tile cutters when my husband pointed this out; they'd broken over two dozen tiles trying to fit them around the faucets. And then they started grumbling loudly to each other about all the time the job was taking. "We're almost doing this for free," Daryl said, and Ray said, "Yeah, it's like doing a welfare job."

THEY NEVER DID grout the tile like they said they would; they simply didn't show up. My husband finished the job. Grouting, hanging cupboard doors, replacing cracked tiles, replacing the toilet (it finally getting hugged by him on the return trip to the bathroom—oh, happy toilet!), and cleaning up the appalling mess they'd left. My husband figured he spent about nineteen hours all told. But the thing was, we still had their tools. Added to Daryl's collection were Ray's: another electric handsaw, three more hand drills, hammers, screwdrivers, and an impressive assortment of nails. We also found Daryl's copy of our signed contract and his rough sketch of our bathroom. We put everything in the trunk of the Peugeot, which, of course, still remained ours. While they were here, they'd never once asked to start it up.

To finish the bathroom we bought some stick-on tiles for the floor, black and white, and two new black towels. The new toilet seat was installed and a new white shower curtain hung from a new chrome curtain rod. A coat of white semigloss paint was applied. The bathroom looked dazzling, even with the crooked tiles. We kept going in there just to marvel at the transformation, to gape and gasp; at last we had a bathroom where our guests would be proud to pee. The only thing missing was one of the doors beneath the sink; Daryl hadn't brought it with him on his last visit.

The final call to Daryl occurred over this issue. It was a Tuesday morning, two weeks after their botched tile job and a full three months after we'd signed the thirty day contract.

MY HUSBAND TOLD HIM we wanted the cabinet door. And asked Daryl when he planned to deliver it. But Daryl started complaining. He said he'd been misled (his word) about the job and my husband said, as a contractor, Daryl should have known what he was getting into. Then my husband mentioned the five hours it had taken him to do the grouting and Daryl said, "Bullshit, ask anybody in the trade, it's only a half-hour job." After this exchange, the "screw yous" and "goddamns" started flying. Also: "you're full of shit," "blow it out your ass" and "who the hell do you think you're talking to?" And then an angry Daryl saying he'd be right out with the door and my husband shouting, "The sooner the fucking better!"

That was six months ago. We haven't heard from Daryl or Ray since. And we still have their tools. And the car. Every one who visits us hears this story and then has a look at the tools in the trunk of the Peugeot. Estimates of their worth run anywhere from five hundred to two thousand dollars, well in excess of the value of the car. Someone suggested that maybe they were stolen. And everyone gives us advice as to what we should do next: sell the tools at a garage sale; send Daryl and Ray a registered letter telling them that we're storing their tools at $2.50 a day; phone up Dr. Donnelly and tell him to never again recommend Tic-Tac-Doe Cabinets; consult a lawyer. And about the tools: it's not unlikely that we'll have them with us for the next several years.

But it's the car that's really the problem: we can't seem to get rid of it. It clings to us like our forlorn toilet demanding to be loved. It costs too much to fix, which is why we've been driving a 1979 Ford Fairmont for the last two years, ever since the Peugeot's head gasket blew on the Pat Bay highway two days before Christmas. We don't think Daryl and Ray still have a claim on the car because they didn't fulfill the terms of the contract.

SO REALLY THIS STORY is one long classified ad: "Peugeot for sale, beautiful body, needs head gasket." If anyone reading this is interested in owning the car we'll let it go for two hundred dollars. Failing that, we have an idea for another ad: "Wanted: door-to-door vacuum salesman. Will trade valuable luxury car for state-of-the-art vacuum cleaner. Only the desperate need apply."

RITARDANDO

IT WAS ANOTHER FAMILY EVENT, one of those huge birthday dinners—Nana's eighty-second—that everyone knocks themselves out for. Fifteen people gathered at our house to eat and drink and hoot it up, and, before the night was out, sing "Happy Birthday" at least a dozen times.

Terry's stylish sisters, Leslie and Jo-Anne, and their husbands, had flown in from Toronto and Calgary and it was always great when his sisters visited because as soon as they arrived they would buy groceries in feast-like quantities, the kinds of things we never had on a regular basis, like a dozen New York strip steaks, and BBQ chickens, and all kinds of snack foods, cheeses, exotic fruits.

And then they bought wine—not two or three bottles carefully chosen with pursed lips and clenched purses—but an entire flamboyant case of vintage French Bordeaux. Plus several flats of beer, and large-sized bottles of gin, vodka, rye and Scotch because Nana liked a *real* drink now and then.

"What do you want?" they'd ask, driving off in their rented car, a Lincoln or a Lexus. "Can we bring you anything back?"

And Terry always said, "Yeah, bring me a fleet of dancing girls." And one time his sisters did that, too, only it was them doing the dancing in their bikini underpants with red and blue balloons attached to their bras—the after-dinner show—and Leslie's husband Ron ran around with the fork from his Swiss Army Knife trying to pop the balloons, only it didn't work, the points were too dull.

SO THE GUESTS ARRIVED and went off shopping. They were laughing as they pulled out of the driveway, rolling down the car window, waving goodbye. Those women were always laughing.

Norman, Jo-Anne's husband, whom everyone agreed was the family eccentric, had driven off with them, too. He'd been put in the back seat and grinned at us like a chauffeured movie star, something he'd told us he wouldn't mind being.

"I wouldn't object to fame," he'd say, seriously, every time he visited. "I wouldn't object at all."

Returning later, the sisters were still laughing and the car trunk was full of food and booze. The rest of us helped carry the bags inside and who could say it wasn't like Christmas? The helping kids went directly for the flats of beer, giving each other significant looks. They were eighteen and twenty-one then but the year before we had lumped them together and declared them grown-up. "We've absolutely had enough," we said. "We're sick of power struggles and worrying about things that are *your* business like are you going to graduate? And are you going to keep that job? Pay your bills? Stay clean and healthy?" Puffing ourselves up, we said, "We're declaring you adults! And we're going to treat you that way, too. Just don't mess up or, like adults, you'll be looking for another cave to dwell in."

"Cool," they said.

WHEN THE RELATIVES VISITED, the kids thought they were in some upscale movie about opulence and good times, in suspended gratification; the *giving* that went on—food, drink, presents, interest. And it was hard for them to resist, hard to act like jerks when their aunts and uncles thought they were so incredibly great. Helping unload those flats of beer, they were no doubt trying to figure out how to scoff a six-pack or two so their friends could come over later, when the birthday party was well under way, and take a lesson with them in how to live really well, how to revel in times of plenty. Why else have these birthday celebrations or Christmases or Easters or anniversaries or any other good news event, we'd decided, if not to do that? And these kids, these exuberant learners, were finding out what motions go into making the good times happen and that was important, too, because we wanted them to learn the *right* motions and to understand about balance.

SO IT WAS NANA'S BIRTHDAY and the party was roaring along well into the night because when Terry's sisters lay on a meal it never begins before 8. And it must have been 10 or 11, during that messy stretch between dinner and dessert, when things heated up. Several bottles of wine had been emptied and Norman began handing out small gifts for the "ladies," and the girls, Anna and Kristy, resplendent in patchy Blondissima hair and nose studs, were beaming while opening their gifts—tiny acorns dipped in gold.

Looking around the table, that old joke suddenly hit me: *It's a tradition in our family. All the women's hair turns blonde at forty.* Because it was blondes to the left of me, blondes to the right.

All these Clairol blondes at one table—it made you think *Swedish.* I said this out loud and Norman hooted, "What about me? I belong to Clairol too!" and Terry shouted, "So do I!"

It was true. He'd succumbed like the rest of us, and in a giddy youth-grabbing gesture had dyed his grey hair blonde.

"I can't tell whether I'm an old guy in need of a face lift or a young guy who looks really bagged," he said of his transformation.

NANA WAS SEATED at the head of the table wearing a long white caftan. She had her huge imitation gold crucifix that must have weighed twelve pounds hanging off her neck, what we call her "armour." Her birthday presents were heaped before her and while she was opening them Leslie told a story. Of how Toronto friends had paid fourteen hundred dollars for a chihuahua puppy that was so small he could fit in the palm of your hand, a small shivery puppy called Juan. They'd had the puppy for two weeks when they went out one Saturday night for dinner and when they returned home they discovered that their cat Noodles had eaten the dog. All that was left was Juan's tiny leg lying on the living room rug. There was no trace of the dog, no blood or anything to indicate he'd met his grizzly end, because the cat had done a really professional job.

"Good thing they found the leg," Leslie said. "Otherwise they'd be going crazy calling and calling and searching everywhere for Juan and not finding him and having sleepless nights thinking he was lost somewhere in the house and would eventually starve to death in a gruesome way."

And Uncle Rickey, the youngest of Nana's four kids, called "Uncle" by everyone, even Nana, because of his hippie beard and ponytail—"He looks like Jesus"—said, "Well, all is not lost, at least now they'll be getting a three-legged stool in the cat box."

"Enough about dogs!" Terry yelled after the laughs, and cranked up the stereo. "Time to dance!"

In a flash Leslie and Jo-Anne had kicked off their shoes and were on the carpet singing along to "Staying Alive," doing all the John Travolta moves. They're both tone deaf, can't sing a note, but this has never stopped them.

Then everyone else was dancing, too. Even Nana, tossing her arthritis aside, even Norman with his chronic lack of rhythm, jerking about the living room like a rapidly deflating balloon. And Terry, whom Nana says could charm the balls off a brass monkey, was at his charming best, jiving expertly with my cousins, Doreen and Shirley, one in either hand. And Anna and Kristy with their minimalist moves, all cool and taut, but in perfect post-Travolta time, enticed a pair of shy uncles, my cousin's husbands, onto the carpet to dance. Even Uncle Rickey, seated on the living room couch with his girlfriend Shelley nestled on his lap, her denim miniskirt bunched at the top of her thighs, was, in his way, dancing, too: grinning serenely, nodding his head to the music. And sitting cross-legged on the floor before his uncle was Bill, looking like a skinny monk doing time before his Buddha.

BEFORE I LEFT THE TABLE to join the dancers I paused. This halting was something I thought of as a "sacred ritardando," a way of being present in the midst of things, a way of both participating in and absorbing the scene before me. Ritardando is a musical term meaning "becoming gradually slower." It's a hesitation, a marking of time. It also means a small island in the middle of movement, a place of regard, contemplation, hallowedness, wholeness. But I like to think it's that place where eternity dwells.

It was a long pause this evening because I was still filled with questions about the unlucky Juan. I couldn't stop myself; I just had to know. Even though I'd laughed along with everyone else when I heard the story about a cat eating a dog. About a leg not much bigger than a toothpick left lying on the living room rug. About fools who pay fourteen hundred dollars for a dog. About the almost universal revulsion for chihuahuas except perhaps in Mexico where nubile senoritas keep them hidden beneath their shawls, safe against their damp breasts, and where cats frequently turn up as entrees, served to unsuspecting tourists fanning themselves in the heat with their guidebooks and believing they're eating authentic Mexican cuisine which, as it turns out, they probably are. Tourists happy to grab a decent meal before taking the rented car to see the sights at Ixtapalapa. And then scouring the Mexican countryside for interesting snapshots, stopping at a roadside shanty discovering poor people and there, amidst the observed squalour, finding a litter of chihuahua puppies squirming in the dirt like large pink maggots.

And did a certain Toronto couple hand over fourteen hundred dollars then and there for a puppy which remained hidden in the man's pocket for the return trip home? And is there a family in Mexico, no longer poor—that fourteen hundred dollars like a lottery win to them and all their relatives—who are now hooting it up at *their* grandmother's birthday celebration because they finally have the necessary funds to likewise be smuggled into the US of A?

And it seems there's no end to this, or to any of our stories.

THE PANELIST

IN THE LATE NINETIES I spent two months in Australia participating in literary festivals, giving readings at universities, and workshops at various state-supported writers' centres. Even if practically no one in the country had heard of me or my books, I was treated (and paid) well. Maybe it wasn't star billing, maybe I had to take the shuttle bus and not a limousine to the festival sites, but the organizers were so generous with per diems and first-class accommodation that I felt I must fulfill the role they had assigned to me; namely, to be part of the "international" filler contingent along with several other international (but otherwise marginally known) writers from Singapore, New Zealand, Scotland, and Malaysia who were doing the festival rounds that season. Our job, it seemed, was to act as literary foliage to the stars, to the heavyweights from Britain and the U.S.—Martin Amis, Anne Rice, P.D. James.

Before the festival season began, I spent two weeks in

Sydney as writer-in-residence at Macquarie University, staying in a university apartment nearby, and eating at the university cafeteria. Returning to the apartment from breakfast one
morning I saw a man standing outside the apartment door
fiddling with a key; I'd seen him at breakfast. We introduced
ourselves. I was carrying a bunch of magenta-coloured flowers that I'd picked from a boulevard tree and he asked if I was
a botanist, appearing disappointed when I said, "No, a writer."

"Oh, well, then, I guess that ends our conversation," he
said. "I'm a physicist. From England. Here doing research."

I felt compelled to speak to him since he was also from
elsewhere. "I feel like an insect dropped out of the sky," I
said, earnestly.

"Yes, well," he said, and before I could explain what I
meant, he hurried away.

I was trying to describe this sense of blindness I was
experiencing, when you can't see your surroundings beyond
what's in front of you, when you can't imagine a landscape,
an environment, because you don't know yet what it is. I was
impatient to know where I was fixed. Other than outside an
ordinary-looking apartment on a busy four-laned road, with
the sun shining down on the strange pine-like trees bearing
magenta blooms.

AT THE END OF THIS STINT my eighteen-year-old daughter Anna arrived
from Canada. She was to spend the next month with me travelling around Australia to the various events where I would
be making an appearance.

Her arrival was the culmination of a year's worth of saving money—hers and ours—plus a year's worth of heated
threats about missing the trip if she "screwed up," i.e. if she
didn't attend school or go to work or was a colossal pain in

the ass to live with. At fifteen she'd been what we now af-
fectionately called "a dissenting adolescent," a wild girl asking only one question of life—"Where's the party!!?" Three
years later she'd mellowed—somewhat—and I was looking
forward to spending a month with her, to "getting my hands
on her," as I put it then.

But only a week before she was due to leave Canada I
received a frantic email from my husband. "She's broken her
ankle!"

Anna had been at one of the several farewell parties her
friends were giving her and jumped across a ditch wearing
platform shoes. The ankle, it turned out, was only bruised
but, even so, my husband decided she needed a pair of flat
shoes for the trip, a decision he soon regretted. "It's taken
two days of shopping," he emailed again, exasperated.

But in the end Anna made it to Australia.

Because her flight landed at 6:30 in the morning and
there were no early buses, I spent forty dollars and took a
taxi to the airport. Anna's plane arrived on time but it was an
hour before she came through the arrival gate. I was certain
her bags were being searched for drugs, and that she was
being roughly handled by Australian customs officials and
refused entry into the country. Looking anxiously through
my address book for the telephone number of the Canadian
consulate, I worried that the office wouldn't be open yet and
that my daughter, crying and bereft, was being held in a basement cell beneath the airport.

I should have known better. This was the girl who made
it possible for us to leave our doors at home unlocked because
every teenage B&E thug in the area was a "personal friend"
of hers. Or so we assumed since, miraculously, during inter-
mittent plagues of local vandalism, our place remained
untouched. Except for the jar of mustard thrown at our front

door one Friday evening. But that was the star student in my husband's behaviour class at the local middle school, a loser wannabe in Anna's estimation.

In any event, she was smiling when she finally walked through Australian customs. Nothing untoward had happened; it was waiting for the luggage that had held things up. We caught a taxi for the return trip to the campus apartment where I'd been staying. Giving the driver the address, I told him the ride would cost no more than forty dollars.

The driver said, "That can't be. There's no way it will cost forty dollars. More like eighty."

My daughter said, "Are you calling my mother a liar?"

I looked at her. A tall girl, she was wearing jeans, sweatshirt and platform running shoes (where were the new shoes?) and held a heavy pack on her lap. Her jaw was clenched and she looked mean. She'd just made a fifteen-hour plane trip and she wasn't taking flak from anyone. And, yes, I ended up paying only forty dollars for the ride.

Once inside the apartment Anna unpacked. She'd brought three illegal substances into the country: two loaves of whole wheat bread, two ears of corn, and a small container of blackberries from our bushes at home.

"A present for you from Dad," she said.

"Weren't you worried about bringing these things through customs?" I asked. There'd been stern warnings in the airport about bringing foodstuffs into Australia—fines, imprisonment.

"A little," she said. "But they didn't look through my bag." She took out her new, flat runners and showed them to me. "Gross, eh?"

"Well, at least you won't hurt your ankle again."

"You guys," she said impatiently. "Like, that was a total overreaction by Dad. Like I'd seriously break my ankle a week before my trip to Australia? Yeah. Right."

We ate the corn and the bread and the blackberries for dinner.

WITHIN DAYS we were on the literary circuit taking a ten-hour train ride through sheep country to Melbourne. Of this trip Anna said dryly, "I liked it. I got to like watching sheep go by. It got so I'd feel excited waiting for another clump of sheep to come into view. I've never seen so many fields of sheep in my life. The time went fast watching all those sheep. It was like being asleep."

The great thing about travelling in Australia, as far as Anna was concerned, was that the drinking age there is eighteen, her age exactly. As soon as she realized this, she phoned her friends at home. "It's awesome!" I overheard her saying. "Like, I can go into all the bars and if anyone tries to ID me, I flash my passport and everything's cool."

She was so pleased about being "legal" that she was constantly trying to buy me drinks. "No," I'd say, attempting some on-the-spot training. "We don't drink beer at 9 in the morning. We wait for lunch or dinner."

But the thing was, she relaxed. Any apprehension she might have had about travelling with me evaporated; she started enjoying herself. Gone was the edgy teenager I'd become used to. Ditto her censoring mother. The fact that we drank beer and wine all over Australia might have had something to do with this.

MY FIRST EVENT of the Melbourne Writers Festival was a morning panel. I left Anna in bed at the hotel and caught the shuttle bus to the festival site. The driver told me he volunteered for the festival because it was a way of getting close to the literary scene.

"But you can't get near the big names," he told me. "They're surrounded by their handlers and travel in limousines. There's no way you could ever talk to a P.D. James or a David Malouf."

Since he had to make do with a lesser name—me—I made a point of chatting him up. Was he an aspiring writer? Who were his favourite writers? P.D. James and David Malouf, he told me curtly. He had never, of course, heard of me.

My panel started at 10 a.m. and was titled: "Short Poppies: Short fiction—the easiest or the hardest to write?"

The panel discussions, I soon learned, were formal affairs. In fact, all appearances at Australian festivals were panel discussions; readings, if they occurred, were rare. As a panelist you were expected to express ideas convincingly and with candour via a prepared "paper" and then participate in a question and answer session with the audience. Worse, for someone used to reading from her work, there was no relying on your work to carry the day. Your work was the last thing the audience was interested in hearing. They lined up to see amusing conversationalists, revered authors. Only if they found you worthy as a personality would they consider buying your book. I wondered if the panels would resemble those TV talk shows from the days of early TV, the kind with dapper old men in bow ties, flamboyant old women in bouffant hairdos. And how were the panelists in Australia chosen, I wondered? A witty speaker with a witless one? The lame with the wild?

I was nervous, and unprepared. I found the greenroom at the venue and went in. The place was empty except for a friendly man who approached me.

"Are you on the panel?" I asked anxiously.

"No, no," he said. "A volunteer. An official greeter. Can I get you anything?"

I had a glass of orange juice and sat down with the idea of looking over my notes. A pair of women came in. One was very young, wearing a black miniskirt and a brown, crushed velvet top, her maroon hair slicked into a ponytail. She was talking excitedly into a cell phone. The other woman was in her late seventies and wore a beige wool coat, flat brown oxfords, and a blue plastic hair band. I turned to this woman and asked, again somewhat desperately, "Are you on the 'Short Poppies' panel?"

"No, I'm not," the woman answered kindly, and I realized that I was speaking to P.D. James.

I quickly consulted the festival program. P.D. James was appearing on a 10 a.m. panel entitled: "Crime Isn't Nearly As Nice As It Used To Be." Three other "international" mystery writers were appearing with her.

The young woman continued talking importantly into the phone. "Yes. I'll see what can be arranged. But I can't promise anything. She's very busy. But if there's any time available I'll give you a ring." She finished her conversation and turned to P.D. James. "That was a woman who said her sister went to school with you. I told her we couldn't fit in a meeting. Is that all right?"

P.D. James said, "Mmmm." She was looking at the festival program and drinking the cup of tea the "official greeter" had brought her.

Seconds later the phone rang again. The conversation sounded much like the earlier one but this time the handler said into the phone, "Could you just hold on a minute?" then whispered to her charge, "This woman says she's related to you. The daughter of your second cousin?"

P.D. James said, "Ask if her mother was Margaret."

The handler did so and nodded in the affirmative. P.D. James then took the phone and said, "Your mother was

Margaret? Yes. Yes. Yes. Yes. Yes. How nice to hear from you. Yes. Yes. I know Sarah but never quite got her acquaintance. It was always very mysterious."

WALKING THROUGH THE CROWD to my event at the Melbourne festival, I met up with two of my fellow panelists. The third, veteran Australian author Amy Witting—*I For Isobel, A Change in the Lighting*—was nowhere to be seen. Then, as we were seated on stage a short, elderly woman in brown slacks and a cardigan, and using a cane, stood up from a front row seat and came towards us. "Amy Witting," she said, sticking out her hand. "I want to go first. I'm a nervous wreck. I hate these panels."

She took her seat on stage and the lights dimmed. "Turn up the damn lights," she bellowed. "I like to see who I'm talking to!"

She began her talk, leaning towards the audience, both hands resting on her cane. She had no notes. "I don't have much to say," she began, and the audience laughed because it appeared she was known as a writer who had a lot to say. "Not much," she continued, "except that short fiction is about the moment. About a particular moment in time. All of my books are about moments. That's all a writer can do—present a believable moment. That's what short stories are. There's nothing mysterious about this. A story is a moment in time and if it's a good story it speaks to all time. A writer must have great curiosity," she continued. "Be prepared to ask questions, to be dissatisfied with surfaces. And great compassion for her characters. And humour. That's very important. If there's no humour, the writing is dead."

Encouraged by Amy Witting, when it was my turn I risked everything—book sales, reputation, audience derision—

and decided to fly in the face of acceptable "panel behaviour." I read short passages from my books, introduced by a few sprinkled comments about the short, short form—dense, poetic, etc. The audience, I was later told, found my rebellious "reading aloud" both shocking and a novel diversion from the usual procedure. (Audience members have the option of filling out assessment "response sheets" after a panel.) Encouraged, I prepared for my upcoming engagements.

ANNA ACCOMPANIED ME to appearances in Wollongong and Sydney, and a week as writer-in-residence in Hobart, Tasmania, where we stayed in an 1803 cottage that was maintained by the Tasmanian Writers' Centre. A squat white structure surrounded by a battered picket fence, it overlooked the harbour and Mt. Wellington in the distance.

As tourists we visited zoos (seventy-two pictures of kangaroos, koala bears and parrots); former penal colonies in Tasmania; saw four movies, all romantic comedies; drank countless cappuccinos (it's difficult to get regular coffee in Australia); and sampled every available brand of Australian beer, several times over. The weather was spring-like—clear and warm—and accompanied by a déjà vu feeling of re-experiencing daffodils, crocuses, and cherry blossoms at the end of August.

Finally, in early September, we stayed with my second cousin, Sheila, and her husband, Jack, in Brisbane, where I was appearing at the Brisbane Writers Festival.

It was here, before the festival events began, that they took us for a day trip on one of Brisbane's river ferries. We'd only met Jack and Sheila twice before, when they'd visited Canada. A retired, well-off couple in their early sixties, they were an energetic and welcoming pair, eager to show us the sights of Brisbane.

But it was not a good day for Anna; she was in a foul mood, sullen and withdrawn, the way she'd been for much of the time during those horrible years from age thirteen to seventeen when her emotions were all over the map. It took me by surprise; I'd become used to the engaging young woman I'd been travelling with, the one who volunteered to carry my luggage, who picked the restaurants we'd eat at and always made the right choice, who pored over guidebooks and made sensible suggestions about bus routes.

I took a group picture while we were waiting to board the river ferry that day and there beside Jack and Sheila, who are smiling and looking relaxed, stands Anna, several feet away, glowering at me for taking the picture.

"What's the matter with *you*?" I managed to hiss out of my cousin's hearing.

She looked at me angrily. "I'm so bored! Brisbane's soooo boring! It's like Disneyland. So germ-free! I can't stand it."

The weather in this faux Disneyland was great, though— hot, clear blue skies, the air heavy with the scent of flowering jasmine. But it made no difference. Anna wore the look of one who's under tenuous control—part hate, part tears. Her disgust for our boring adult lives was palpable and it's hard not to sound inane when there's someone like that in your midst judging your every move and utterance.

Without acknowledging Anna's black mood, though, the rest of us carried on bravely.

Sheila: Isn't it a wonderful day!

Me: This is so pleasant riding around on the ferry, getting off, having coffee, having lunch. Look at all the palm trees!

Jack: That development over there is called Riverside. It was built in 1991 and is a very popular place.

Sheila: Look at all the Wattle trees! They're my favourite trees. I love trees!

Jack: At one time the area along the river was used for industry. But now some of those old buildings have been made into apartments. They're pretty expensive.

Me: This is so great seeing the city like this. What a fabulous form of public transportation!

Sheila: People are so clever. Look at that bridge. Imagine building something like that!

Jack: It's a really interesting thing, the way they make brick. It's quite a long procedure. First they...

THE TOPIC OF MY FIRST PANEL at the Brisbane festival was: "I Know Funny—Do We All Laugh at the Same Things?" I'd planned to say a few words and then read something from my latest book, as I had done in Melbourne.

The event was held in the outdoor River Tent at the Queensland Cultural Centre, a sprawling collection of libraries, auditoriums and museums fronting the Brisbane River. Admission to the festival was free; otherwise, as I was told by one of the organizers, no one would come. An audience of two hundred, including uniformed schoolboys, waited for the 4:30 panel to begin.

On the panel with me were standup comic Richard Stubbs, two writers from *Good News Week*, an Australian TV show celebrated as "zany and irreverent," and feminist cartoonist Judy Horacek. Just before we took our seats on the platform, Richard Stubbs, who was acting as chair, gathered us together in a loose circle where we all said "Hep!" like football players about to sprint onto the field.

Richard Stubbs opened the proceedings and was, of course, brilliant. I remember little of what he said. But everyone laughed. He'd just had his first book published, *Still Life*, a book of comic riffs. On the cover he's dressed like the Mona Lisa and looking very much like the original. He told the audience that he didn't have a clue what made people laugh; you were either funny or you weren't and he said this in such a way that people were wiping tears from their eyes.

I looked alarmingly at my notes on medieval fools and postmodern dislocation and started to feel sick. This was not an audience who'd warm up to deconstruction theory.

The next panelists, the writers for the TV show, were also brilliant—a kind of Laurel & Hardy pair, except they were both the goofy one. TV couldn't have typecast them any better: tall, skinny, nerdy, long haired, bespeckled, maybe twenty-nine or thirty, wearing soiled T-shirts and big black boots like the *Keep on Truckin'* characters in *Zap comix*. Both of them said straight off that they didn't have a clue what made people laugh. "There's no definition," one of them declared and poured water down the front of his shirt. The audience roared. The other had a joke about Pablo Neruda and the business of putting poetry on the busses: "What does a Pablo Neruda bus horn sound like?" he asked the audience. "Neruuuda. Neruuuda." The uniformed school boys in the front row laughed their heads off.

By now my notes were soaked with perspiration. I looked about wildly for an escape route, for someone to save me, thinking: I shouldn't be here; there's been a terrible mistake; I'm going to throw up.

Judy Horacek, next up, was even funnier than the three guys. She'd just published *Lost in Space*, a book of cartoons. She also said she didn't know what humour was so had looked the word up in the Oxford dictionary. "Humour: Antic wit, comedy, drollery, fun" and so on. The audience found the list very funny.

She then talked about her cartoons. About fridge magnets leaping off fridge doors—"Suicide of the fridge magnets;" about Mick Jagger in science class—"So tell us about oxygen, Michael." "It's a gas, gas, gas." About cell phones going feral. About Santa Claus on the shrink's couch: "It doesn't matter what other people think—it's important to believe in yourself." And the philosophy of the dodo bird: "Life's a bitch and then you're extinct."

As it was nearing my turn, I considered getting up from my chair, announcing to the audience, "I'm not funny," and walking away from the platform in a dignified manner. The other panelists had, one after the other, worked the audience into a quivering, almost hysterical state. Expectations were running high. Was everyone expecting a giant laugh orgasm by the time it was my turn? Some kind of fulfilled release? So that afterwards, during the question and answer period, we could all get relaxed and cozy and satisfied together and say things like, "Wasn't *that* good!" and "Whew! What a workout!"

What a downer, as we used to say in the sixties when the dope got flushed down the toilet: "The cops are coming!" (They never did.) What a downer! Panelists leaping off the panelist platform: "Suicide of the Unfunny Ones." Panelists contemplating the Philosophy of the Unfunny Panelist: "Life's a joke and then your mind goes blank." The Unfunny Panelist on the analyst's couch: "Honest, Doc, it was supposed to be literary fiction."

What did I do? I read half a page from my notes: "The fool was a revered and feared personage in Medieval times." (The audience fearing boredom.) I read something from my books (Heh, heh.) I kept it short. (Thank god, bring back the comedians.)

Later I looked up "fool" in the *Macquarie Encyclopedic*

Thesaurus. The associative words included: ass, birdbrain, boob, dickhead, fuckwit, nutcase, turkey, and wacker.

Ah, no wonder then! What a fuckwit I'd been.

Mick Jagger at Panelist School: "So tell us about 'funny,' Michael." "It's an ass, ass, ass."

DURING THIS SESSION, Anna was sitting in the audience at first but after Richard Stubb's performance she wandered to the grass area at the front of the tent. I watched as she and a six-foot-tall uniformed schoolboy shared a cigarette. "Ah, she's missing people her own age!" I thought from my prison at the panelists' table—relief at realizing there was a reason for her former moodiness.

"He's invited me to a movie tonight," she told me later. "I'll take a taxi. I won't be late." And then, throwing me a crumb, said, "You were pretty good up there today. The other ones weren't *that* funny. But you should stick to giving readings, Mom. Seriously. That's where you do best."

"We should put *you* on a panel," I told her. "A panel of writers' children."

"Yeah, that'd be cool. I could tell about all the readings you made me go to. Remember the Denman Island Poetry Festival and that nude performance guy? That was so gross the way he jumped over our chairs. What a view! They should do that here."

I WAS FEELING MORE CONFIDENT about the Sunday morning panel, "Words That Define a Generation," because after the humour panel on Friday afternoon I'd spent most of Saturday feverishly rewriting my notes. I was prepared for anything. I had five sheets of paper and was going to read from them like an academic. "This is a difficult topic, one that is at the heart of the writer's dilemma today," I would begin, carrying through remorselessly to my closing comments about the "writer as performing seal."

I told Sheila and Jack optimistically, "You'll want to get there early, the place will be packed."

The panel was to be held in the auditorium, the festival's largest venue. My relations were from the stern world of banking and business and this was to be their first-ever literary event.

In the green room before the panel began I met up with my co-panelists: Mark Davis, the chair, Sean Condon, and Michael Wilding, one of Australia's leading fiction writers and one whose work I very much admired. At fifty-five, he looked nothing like the radical politico pictured on his covers, but more like a master at a private school—grey flannels, tweed jacket, soiled white shirt. The group of us sipped water and tried to relax.

Sean Condon, the young Australian author of *Sean & Dave's Long Drive* and *Drive Thru America* pulled at his collar and said as we were heading towards the stage, "Oh god! I feel like a piece of shit. I don't know what I'm going to say. I'm too stupid. I shouldn't be here. There's been some terrible mistake. I shouldn't be on this panel. I don't have a single thing to say. I'm going to throw up." He was wild-eyed and sweating heavily.

The auditorium was half-full. Or half-empty depending on your anxiety level. About one hundred people if you counted the sound man and the festival staff standing by the door. Anna and our relatives sat midway in the audience.

After a few introductory words from Mark Davis, it was Sean Condon's turn. He wiped his brow, shakily poured himself some water, cleared his throat, and sipped his water

again. "I don't know why I'm here," he began. "I'm too stupid to be on a panel. I don't know anything." The audience
laughed. Particularly enthusiastic were a large group of
young women in the front rows, his fans. "I've made some
notes," he stammered, "on the back of this bookmark..."
And he held it up. More laughs. He continued in this vein
for fifteen minutes and managed to convey to the audience
that while his generation might be terminally confused, it definitely had an edge on what makes people laugh. There was
loud applause when he finished.

Both Michael Wilding and I read from our prepared
texts, Michael focusing on the political climate within which
literature gets written, and me on postmodernism and the
writer's dilemma: write and/or perform? Competent,
thoughtful presentations but hardly a laugh fest.

Sean Condon fielded most of the questions during the
session afterwards. Everyone wanted to hear what he had to
say: "Well, shit, I dunno...."

Afterwards, I asked Sheila, "What did you think?"

"I thought that first speaker, Sean something, was dreadful," she said. "The way he said the F-word to that journalist
asking that question." (Middle-aged journalist with a mock
question full of indecipherable postmodern terminology to
which Sean Condon answered, "In the words of my generation, fuck off." I laughed along with everyone else.) My cousin
continued. "I've never heard such language in public! That
journalist's very well known. He's often on the ABC, you
know. And to be treated that way in public. It was awful!"

Jack beside her nodded gloomily.

"That's nothing," Anna declared. "You should go to a
Canadian reading." And she quoted her favourite line from
a Sheri-D Wilson performance piece. Right there on the
crowded sidewalk, in the dazzling Brisbane sunshine, she

stood back and bellowed: "Don't fuck with a fuck!"

Our relatives blanched. It was too much for them. They both shuddered, then hurried away for reviving cappuccinos. Anna and I headed for the beer garden; Michael Wilding soon joined us.

"I'LL BUY," said my take-charge daughter. And went into the refreshment tent.

Michael and I found a table outside on the grass and sat down beneath the black and white Bollinger umbrella. Beside us ferry boats sped by on the Brisbane River.

While we waited for Anna, Michael asked me how travelling with a teenage daughter had been.

"Pretty good," I said. "But it'll be better for both of us later. In the memory of it. In the retelling."

"You mean there'll be a book?"

"Who knows?" I said.

When Anna returned with our drinks, I was struck by how beautiful she looked, sophisticated. Her blonde hair was pulled into a low bun and she was wearing sunglasses. She could have been twenty-five years old. She asked Michael, "Do you know Sean Condon?" By now Sean was holding court with a group of young women at a nearby table.

Michael said, "Vaguely."

"Could you ask him over?" she said, taking a sip of her beer. "I'd like to talk to him about his book. I liked the way he talked. And I want to ask him how he did that. Travelled around a country and then wrote a book about it. That'd be an awesome thing to do. Yeah. That'd be *so* cool."

MAN IRONING

AT THE DINNER TABLE I was yapping away: "I'm glad I was born in the twentieth century. As a woman. A century of huge strides for women in the Western world blah blah blah..."

I'd spent the afternoon in an apron and didn't want the men in my life getting the wrong idea. Making dinner was something I *chose* to do and wearing an apron merely an expedient against unnecessary laundry. I think they believed it. So I was yapping away.

My husband looked up from his vegetarian pizza, already miffed because it was a vegetarian pizza and not a moose or something on his plate, and said, dryly, "Yes, any other time you would have been burnt at the stake."

Our twenty-three-year-old son, Bill, had come over for supper, and he laughed at my husband's comment, shocked and pleased, like it was a "right on!" moment, another point scored for the Neanderthal male. Giddily role-modelling on his father's endearing crankiness, he was chuckling away like anything, having a tiny vacation from reality. I love that Bill's new live-in girlfriend, Faye, is a feminist and that Bill now spends a good deal of time washing dishes and vacuuming, grocery shopping and agonizing over meal plans. Only last year, when he still lived at home, we'd regularly lose him under a mound of dirty laundry, but now all that's changed. It's amazing what love can do in the clean socks, clean teeth department. I give the girl full credit for his transformation. I could only manage the theory part. Stunningly, she's achieved application.

Because of this change in Bill, I was pleased that he arrived to find his father ironing jeans in the kitchen. It was like a New Age affirmation. And ironing on a Saturday afternoon, as well, when there were hardware stores to wander about in, or bikes to tinker with in his shed.

There were three pairs of jeans stacked on the kitchen table, waiting their turn. Two more hung on hangers from a chair. My husband was laboriously finishing work on another pair, tongue protruding, eyes narrowed in concentration. He'd been ironing for an hour and a half. That worked out to thirty minutes for one pair of jeans. It was painful to watch. Creases were redone and waistbands were meticulously positioned. Using a three-foot carpenter's ruler, he measured the crease line from the side seam, taking notes for future reference. He spent an inordinate amount of time adjusting the controls on the iron, monitoring the water level, spitting on the iron to check for sizzle. I watched him compulsively smoothing and re-smoothing the ironing board cover. Wasn't there a recent book by a neurosurgeon about idiot savants? I wondered. It was hugely popular. I made a mental note to look for it next time I was in the local library.

As for my husband's ironing, I couldn't help him. After twenty-seven years of ironing dominance by me, he'd declared he was taking over. My private response, naturally, was one of elation, of satisfied accomplishment. It had taken me twenty-seven years of bad ironing to effect this dazzling change, a long and determined haul, it's true, but then boys raised in the fifties were spoiled with faulty domestic training and came to expect such things. His mother ironed *everything*, including his baseball hat and his jock strap.

My husband irons his jeans because he requires a rigid crease down each leg and because when I've done the job his jeans have creases that travel from thigh to ankle in an erratic zigzag, like a crease on amphetamines. He said that wearing such crazily ironed jeans made it hard for him to stand up straight and that people kept leaning to the side when they talked to him. So now he primly does the job himself. The resultant creases are military precise, good enough for a parade.

I have to admire his dedication. But mostly what I admired that day was the stage set—my husband ironing in the kitchen, the newly-trained vacuuming son returning home to find his father in the throes of a dogged domesticity. The scene was like a reverse stage play from the rigid fifties and I wished I had a laptop on the kitchen counter, a pile of excellent first pages stacked beside it while the oppressed-for-art-supporting spouse slaved away and I created my brains out. Like Harold Pinter. Or Tennessee Williams. With washing strung on a line between us, and steam heat fogged windows. With a smelly baby or two squalling from the corner.

Instead, equally domestic and apron-clad, I was chopping mushrooms and green peppers for the pizza. The baby, full-grown and eating pretzels, was sprawled on the couch reading *Brave New World* by Aldous Huxley and enjoying a brief vacation from feminism while awaiting his supper.

At this juncture, his father was unaware that a culinary storm cloud was looming on the horizon: the pizza was going to be vegetarian. If he was dreaming of T-bone steaks or pizza stacked with nitrate-laced salami, I had no way of knowing. What I did know was that his mind was temporarily at rest about turkey soup.

Earlier in this ironing day he'd become alarmed when he'd smelled boiling bones. "What's that?" he cried.

"Turkey soup for tomorrow." I was proud that after ten months I'd finally got around to the frozen bones from last Christmas.

"Turkey soup?" he cried even louder. "Are you insane? Do you not realize that Thanksgiving is a week away? That next week and for countless coming weeks it will be turkey soup and nothing but turkey soup?"

It hadn't occurred to me. Next week is next week.

"Don't you like turkey soup?" I blithely asked. You'd think that after all these years I'd have the answer to that question. But then he was surprised to recently discover that, along with brushing my teeth before bed, I applied deodorant.

"I loathe, despise, and revile turkey soup," he hissed in a red-faced, taut neck cord kind of way, belabouring the point, I thought. Apoplectic?

"The smell of boiling bones makes me want to puke," he continued. "My gag reflex goes non-stop. Turkey soup makes me want to leave home, take a sudden trip to visit my sister in Toronto where all they eat are barbecued ribs and New York steaks. You know the last time I had barbecued ribs? 1991!"

"But you had a pork chop last Tuesday," I said, laying the groundwork for the vegetarian pizza. "And you said you were interested in trying vegetarian food."

"I take a glance at one of your health food books and now I'm to be drawn and quartered?"

Tactfully, I let the matter sit for a few minutes before returning to the subject of turkey soup. "I suppose I could freeze the bones for another time," I said in the spirit of conciliation.

"Freeze boiled bones? Are you out of your mind? Are we that hard up you have to make a career out of boiling and re-boiling bones? And it's none of the white meat, either," he added, petulantly. "It's all wings and drumsticks. You know I hate dark meat."

Once again I marvelled at how much of my day revolves around things domestic—instead of creating additional theories of evolution that might be of interest to the likes of Richard Dawkins; instead of creating beautifully sculpted forms out of found domestic objects that would bedazzle someone like artist Andy Goldsworthy—I spend my days dreaming up the many *creative* ways to make a turkey last several months.

I had to lie down.

Between boiling bones and chopping green peppers, I took to the couch in rebellion, grabbing the nearest thing to read—my husband's latest issue of *Health and Social Behavior.* Amazingly, like some sinister cosmic message, the lead study carried the headline: "Unequal Share of Housework Causes Depression in Women."

I wondered if I was depressed. According to this study, I should be, and massively so. Apparently, married men reported sharing 37% of household labour while married women, whether working outside the home or not, reported doing twice as much—over 75%. Not only that, but marriage actually increased the workload for women: fourteen hours per week more than their unburdened single sisters. For married men versus single men, it was only ninety minutes more. Around here that translates into three pairs of ironed jeans.

But I couldn't get inflamed reading the stats. Or depressed. Once I might have, but not any longer. Some years back I abandoned the hysterical tally sheet—me cook, you take out the garbage—in deference to my husband's ability to fix broken washing machines and lawnmowers; paint houses; prune trees; sell beater cars at higher prices than we paid for them; entertain, then evict door-to-door canvassers, and so on. And now to that sterling list I've added: irons his jeans.

But back to the dinner table, that reliable old scene of domestic carnage. It was vegetarian pizza night and my husband was pouting at me from across the table, nibbling on a piece of burnt pineapple. Clearly, after three hours of steady ironing he was worn out.

Bill, though, was eating robustly. He's a health food convert (Faye's influence, again) but once he was a young man who travelled with his own bags of jalapeño potato chips. Now he negotiates life with a bottle of flaxseed oil and a container of soft tofu. In his male solidarity days he was a dedicated meat-and-potatoes boy. My husband loved those times, the two of them out on the deck barbecuing steaks the size of small steers. They would wear that meat, blood on their lips, fat on their chins, animal antibiotics rampaging through their bloodstreams like killer cowboys. While inside Anna and I pecked virtuously at a bean and rice casserole.

Until a return of those happy days, though, my husband has become the victim of a semi-vegetarian household, abandoned to the occasional piece of meat, eaten alone and grumpily like an old lion trying to mine sustenance from a frozen hamburger patty.

We went to bed early that night. My husband, exhausted from ironing (and possibly meat deprivation) was soon asleep, his right hand slapping the covers, still at work at the ironing board in the steamy kitchen of his subconscious, it seemed.

Lying awake, I wondered about the mechanics of being burnt alive at the stake, about the division of labour and how the male/female percentages would tally up. What would the studies say about that? Would both sexes gather the wood for the fire or would it be something irate husbands alone would enjoy, tossing the triumphant match at the feet of their bound, and no longer domineering, wives?

I next thought about the domestic sculptures I could make out of ironing boards, turkey legs, and abandoned vegetarian pizzas. And then about the scholarly paper I could write. In it I would detail my new theory of the mutant jean-ironing gene that I'd recently discovered. I'd explain how these genes were currently replicating like crazy among the male population of the species. I'd have graphs and statistics and everything.

THE BAR BURNS DOWN

RICKEY'S TURNING FIFTY. Everyone says, Five-oh? Rickey? Who woulda thunk? Still wearing his peace sign.

Then the bar burns down on the eve of his party.

Nana cries. "Poor Rickey! When he was born he was yellow all over. Never did have any luck in this world."

The rest of us have a good laugh. "Bad luck, no way! An old hippie finding love and business on a beautiful Gulf Island? He and Shelley managing a bar, a motel, a marina?"

"Well, he's not managing very well." Nana says. "The bar burned down."

We tell her it wasn't his fault. The cook tossed a cigarette into a pile of garbage out back of the bar. The cook's an idiot. There you go. We tell her what's *not* managing well is Shelley's sixteen-year-old daughter announcing she's having a baby—next Sunday. And the party's Friday night. A pudgy girl, she'd hidden her belly behind oversized shirts. The father's one of the short-order cooks in the bar's adjoining restaurant.

"Oh, boy," Nana says. "What does that make me? Some kind of great grandma?

"Step-great-grandma," we say. "Once removed."

THEN WE SAY, so what if the bar burned down? We'll have the party anyway. We'll be moral support. Nothing like a party to cheer things up.

So the trip to Rickey's place is on. Eight of us wait in the ferry lineup—Nana and her three other kids, two spouses, one son, one dog, both ours. It's the day of Rickey's actual birthday, Friday, September 17th. We'll get to his island by noon.

The flown-in relatives—sisters Leslie and Jo-Anne, and Jo-Anne's husband Norman—have rented a Lincoln. Nana rides up front. "No sense in looking poor," she tells us, one of her all-purpose lines.

Norman, wearing an olive green Armani suit, has brought a sleek stainless-steel Thermos filled with manhattans. Also a separate container of stemmed maraschino cherries and a martini glass that travels in a special velvet-lined box. Norman is sixty-eight, a retired architect, lately to be seen in Calgary TV commercials.

"An event full of drama and emotion," he says of the burned down bar. "It'd be a good piece for my improv class. But I'm no good at improv. I don't know what it is. I'm too wooden, too stiff. I never come across any other way. It's a real problem. But put me in a commercial for a real estate development where I have to walk through a house and look in cupboards and I shine."

"Shine all the way to the bank, you mean," says Nana.

"Well, yes," Norman says, pleased.

(Dry manhattan: 2 shots rye or Irish whiskey; 1 shot Italian vermouth; 2 dashes Angostura Bitters. Times 8 for a 30 ounce Thermos. Serve in a martini glass with one stemmed maraschino cherry).

TERRY AND I DRIVE the old Toyota hatchback with our son Bill and dog Mutz wedged into the back seat. The dog's thirteen, hangs over our shoulders panting her hot vile breath. Open the windows! Tell her to lie down!

I've just had a book published and have copies with me. Waiting for the ferry, Norman takes a book and heads for the craft booths. Everyone follows. If he wore a cape you'd think he was Oscar Wilde.

He shows the book to a girl selling jewellry. "This is my sister-in-law's book." Pointing me out. "And this is her husband. And this is her dog."

The girl yawns. "Oh, yeah?"

Tourists give us interested looks.

Norman turns to me to instruct. "It's all about promotion," he says grandly. "People have to know you're a star. Otherwise. Pfffft."

My husband laughs. "No sense in looking anonymous."

Nana asks, "Is the book about me?"

THEN WE'RE ON the small ferry snapping pictures. It's a warm day, the sun's out, postcard weather. Nana's wearing blue and white, and a nautical hat like the captain on *The Love Boat*. We stand on the open car deck with our cameras. Take one of the group! That sailboat! That bird! Take one of the Lincoln! The dog!

"Take one of me," says Norman. "I need some new head

shots." Posing, he worries about the angle of his head, his posture, the harshness of the sun. "I've got to look young. Casting directors won't hire you if you're over sixty. Unless you're Sean Connery, of course." Then he inspects the shots that have been taken. "Oh, delete that one. Look how I'm standing. I look like a bird of prey."

The green and blue scenery sliding by.

WHEN WE ARRIVE we find the burned-down bar is only burned-out. It's standing. The restaurant hasn't been touched by the fire, though it's closed. This is all mildly disappointing. The catastrophe is only half a catastrophe. There's a hole in the roof of the bar; it's blackened inside, and surrounded by red and yellow tape now that the fire marshall's involved.

Rickey and Shelley droop before us. Tall and thin, they look like marionettes with their strings gone slack. They've been up all night, look stunned and dishevelled. Shelley's slept in her long print skirt. Her hair's uncombed; she's barefoot. How come? They ask. Why us? Circles under their eyes. Rickey's got bits of toast in his beard; he's holding a can of beer. We realize, for them, it's a full catastrophe, nothing half about it. It's the direct hit, the hamburger with everything on it.

Rickey says, "The booze was destroyed, maybe we should cancel the party."

Shelley says, "Willow's baby. I had no idea. What if it comes tonight?"

Nana says, "Whoo boy."

Norman asks, "Where are the owners?"

"California," says Rickey. "But they're cool. There's insurance. And they wanted to redo the bar anyway."

"Well then," we say. "It's not the end of the world! It's

your birthday! A marker! A party! A baby! Nothing to do but laugh it up. Have a good time."

We're given motel rooms, and then drive to the village for wine, beer, cheese, jalapeño chips, juice. And a look in the gift shops at the Seaweed Mall.

Rickey and Shelley head off for a nap.

DURING THE AFTERNOON a couple of off-duty waitresses get to work setting up tables and umbrellas, attaching red, yellow, and blue balloons to the wire fence surrounding the motel pool where the party will happen. When they're finished it looks like the stage set for a wedding. Then a friend of Rickey's called Too Tall Ed arrives and parks his pickup beside the fence and guides his piano down a ramp, then wheels it across the cement surround to a corner by the pool. He'll spend the evening playing.

Around 4 o'clock people start arriving—all of Rickey and Shelley's friends, most of them permanent Islanders. The men wear jeans and baseball caps and red and black plaid flannel shirts. The women wear thin dresses and open-toed shoes or else jeans and runners with soles as thick as truck tires. Everyone drinks beer out of cans or wine out of clear plastic cups. Leslie and Jo-Anne in their crisp white slacks and embroidered sweaters, and Norman in his Armani suit holding his martini glass aloft like the Olympic torch so it won't get knocked by the crowd, mingle with the flannel-shirted Islanders as if this were a sales convention and they're working the crowd.

Every guest has brought a dog. Or so it seems. They're large, pushy dogs and run in packs having a party of their own, scouring the place for food, new smells. They have names like Cheemo, Bear, Bandit, Cody, Shyla.

Mutz is worn out from being sniffed at, from having to ward them off.

AT 6:30 DINNER IS SERVED. The guests line up before the single barbecue for hamburgers and Caesar salad made by a rookie cook who is not the cigarette tosser, nor the father of Willow's child. He's young, maybe nineteen, nervous about his debut performance as "chef of the evening." His white chef's hat's too big, keeps slipping down on his forehead; his chef's jacket is smeared with grease. Pretty soon he's sweating, becomes snarly when he can't keep up with the hamburger demand, when he runs out of Caesar salad.

(Caesar salad for 100: 25 heads of romaine lettuce, shredded; 14 litre can of Caesar salad dressing; 4 boxes of croutons.)

SO THERE'S THE SCENE—night's falling; there's a blue and orange sky; a warm breeze, early stars, the moon's full. And Nana's standing beside Too Tall Ed, a drink in her hand, leaning on the piano like she was an admirer of Gershwin. She's making requests, singing along. "Danny Boy." "New York, New York." "It Was Just One of Those Things." Which could be the anthem for the party.

Rickey's standing around drinking beer, a crowd of his pals nearby. Everyone's laughing about the fire. "Who woulda thunk?" "A mind blow, or what?" Rickey's happy now, relaxed, receiving gifts—baseball hats, a T-shirt that says "Fifty Ain't Old," a box of Havana cigars, several bags of grass. Along with a new sweatshirt that we know will be wrecked within a week because he'll wear it to change the oil in his truck, we give him a picture. It's of a younger Rickey and represents, we think, his idea of Heaven. In the picture he's twenty-five years old, full-bearded and dreamy-eyed, and lying in a hammock grinning, surrounded by six-foot-tall marijuana plants.

Down on the beach there's a bonfire. Guests keep disappearing. You turn around and wonder where everyone's gone. Then turn around again and the party's full of people, laughing louder than ever.

A cloud of pungent smoke drifts along the tide line.

THE PREGNANT WILLOW wanders around with a can of Coke. She's getting plenty of hugs from the Islanders; everyone thinks the news about the baby is great. Since her announcement she's been living in a trailer with her boyfriend, the short-order cook. Out back of Rickey's and Shelley's place. They fixed it up in a rush, they said, made it homey for the kids. The boyfriend's at the party someplace, but we haven't met him yet.

"It's like the Ozarks," Norman says of the living arrangements. He's pouring himself another manhattan. "All that fetid closeness. Cheers."

"It's like that PBS show, *The Darling Buds of May*," says his wife. She clinks his glass with her wine. "The one with all the chickens and kids."

Willow says she's naming the baby Fabio, after the WWF wrestler. "That's the name," she says. "Boy or girl, it don't matter to me."

Willow's round face and belly are like a second full moon hanging over the party.

BILL'S NEW BAND—Thunder Sauce—had been hired to play at Rickey's party for seven hundred and fifty dollars plus accommodation and meals and everyone in the band was pumped, their highest-paying gig ever. They told their friends, put posters up around Sidney giving ferry schedules to the Island, info about sleeping beside the bar. There was a rumour of a girl coming from two hundred miles away because word had gotten out. Now the gig is off because of the fire. Too Tall Ed's their replacement. A bummer for the band, and more of a bummer when we hear the ferry horn bellowing from three miles away. Because carloads of young people soon roar down the driveway to the Island Bar & Marina, and each car unloads six or seven kids with packs and sleeping bags and cases of beer so that all together there must be over a hundred of them.

This crowd is hungry for live music and, we fear, could turn mean, and it's all our fault, Terry's and mine, because it's our son who's got them here and the line of responsibility leads to us. But Bill is calm. He saunters towards the advancing crowd and explains the way things are, and everyone says "No way?" And then three quarters of them elect to take the last ferry at 9:30 because there's a party in Sidney that won't even start till 12.

BY 10 O'CLOCK we're in one of the motel rooms having a last drink, the rest of the party-goers still hanging around the pool where Too Tall Ed keeps playing. It's "Proud Mary" now, and Bo Diddley, and hits from Fleetwood Mac. People are dancing, whooping it up. Someone, naturally, falls in the pool.

We, the relatives, have taken all kinds of pictures, especially ones of the sisters and Nana standing around the piano, the marina boats in the backdrop. And of Rickey grinning amongst his friends. Norman is lying on the pullout bed in the motel living room drinking a last manhattan, and Mutz, exhausted, climbs onto his lap.

Norman makes a good show of enduring the dog and balancing his drink while Jo-Anne and Leslie serve out snacks, including the most uniformly made potato chip in existence. They come in a cylinder container and fit into each other like plastic deck chairs.

(Pringles: Buy them at any grocery store.)

LESLIE HAS GIVEN Nana a pill so everyone can get some sleep because Nana wanders in the night. She's been put in the main bedroom but doesn't want to go to bed. She's eighty-seven years old and enjoying herself, and it's true she's had too much to drink and keeps repeating, "I just want to say how special I think everyone is and that I love you all very much," going from person to person in the motel room wearing pink sweatpants now, and bare feet.

While we're relaxing, Jo-Anne tells us how to freeze green grapes. She says they make an excellent after-dinner nibble, like sorbet to clear the palette, but with much less work.

"When you eat them," she says, "they taste cold, and are light green and glowing. Like something from outer space."

(Frozen grapes: Put single green grapes on a plate and place them in the freezer.)

The following Sunday, after we've left Rickey's island, Willow has her baby, right on schedule, just as she'd said. It's a girl, eight pounds, two ounces, with a head covered in red fuzz. She calls her baby Fabina.

After a couple months the short-order cook moves off; it's all too much for him. But Willow doesn't seem to mind; the cook did his job and now he's not needed.

Willow turns out to be a doting, capable mother. "I hate school anyway," she says. "Now I can stay home and no one will bug me."

As for Fabina, everyone agrees she is one lucky baby. She's the latest member of the Island tribe, a large, close-at-hand, laid-back family. One of the Islanders gives her a red and black flannel shirt for a baby present. It looks just like the grown-up version but is made to size.

When we see her a few weeks later, Willow, delighted, shows it around. "Is that awesome," she grins, "or what?"

THE JUDGE

"THE JUDGING SHOULDN'T take too much of your time," the magazine editor said. "There'll be a load of entries, but we'll whittle it down to a hundred or so."

I did some quick figuring: one hundred stories at a maximum of five thousand words each. If I read quickly, say at thirty minutes per story, it should take about fifty hours. And that's just the first go-round. There'd be second readings, and a third. Then the long deliberation over the winners and the honorable mentions. I estimated that judging the contest would take half the month of August.

"We can't pay you," the editor said. "But you'll get a little write-up in the magazine when the winners are announced."

Naturally I said yes. A "little write-up," no matter how small, is something few writers can afford to dismiss; the thin acknowledgement might result in a book sale. One. To your cousin in Ottawa.

But there were further reasons for saying yes.

The American humorist Garrison Keillor came to mind. He agreed to judge a poetry contest to save his country— from the "glum and pretentious reflections" that usually win contests and then are served up to innocent school children as examples of the poet's craft. "Barns of boredom," he called the anthologies.

I like that. Saving the country for literature, saving innocents. I also liked the idea that this contest was "blind," meaning that author's names would not be attached to the stories. Judges are sometimes "blind," too, a fact that doesn't go unnoticed by unsuccessful entrants.

In any case, I've come to not mind judging contests. I feel I'm doing some good in the world, promoting literature, helping the worthy along. I look upon it as volunteer work, like collecting for the Heart and Stroke Foundation. Maybe a touch better than that, because going door to door last February I felt like a vagrant. One man spoke for half an hour about his new Airstream trailer, then rummaged in his pocket and gave me four quarters. A woman at a house two streets over who has a sign outside advertising electrolysis— a cartoon woman astride a giant chin pulling on a hair the size of a baseball bat—told me to get off her property. She flung open her door when I was halfway up her driveway. "I'm collecting for the Heart and Stroke Foundation," I called brightly. "I don't care if you're collecting for King bloody Tut!" she yelled, and went back inside. I quit canvassing later that day when an old man with an awful look in his eye answered the door naked. "Come in," he grinned. "I'm just making the cocktails."

So there you have it: judging writing contests is preferable to collecting door to door. You're hidden away while you do your good work. There's not an annoying neighbour in sight, only a tall stack of stories on your desk, each one calling to you sweetly, "Choose me!"

Judging contests is safer, too. I've yet to hear of a judge receiving a lewd invitation from an unsuccessful entrant, though many might be looking for that kind of thing as a perk.

If the judging of writing contests were televised the commentary would be intense and given in hushed tones, like commentaries for billiards, bowling, or cricket.

"She's put on her glasses. She's taken up her pen. She's reading. She's continuing to read. Still reading. Ah! A story has been flung to the floor. What do you think, Margaret? The yes or the no pile?"

Every entrant is hoping that you, as a representative of the literary universe, will bestow upon them the great affirmative nod, the handhold up the literary ladder. William Blake has a drawing about that. Not the famous one with the god figure reaching from a cloud, but the one with the couple trying to climb to the moon. They've got a long ladder pointed at the moon and they've actually started climbing. It's William Blake's version of *Climb Every Mountain*. It's William Blake being funny.

A writing judge must have a sense of humour, too. Because it's tough work. There are long hours of reading. There is worry about the authors' personal lives, the possibility that the stories of marriage breakup, alcoholism, parent's death, or the poignant demise of pets may be autobiographical.

There is also the restraint a judge must exercise not to edit or rewrite the submissions or, in rare cases, lift a story idea. The humour part comes after the winners have been picked. It's a kind of light-headed, zany release, affording an occasion to celebrate—something that judges of writing contests, like normal people, are continually on the prowl for. I imagine that judges of cat and dog shows feel the same way:

the satisfactory sweat of a job well done, the cold beer, the shoes kicked off.

By and large, writing judges take their jobs seriously. It's an unfortunate myth that winners are decided by coin toss or by spouses, or children. Because the judges of writing contests are professionals. Most have entered contests at some time themselves. Some still do. (We know who we are.) They realize what's at stake—anguish and hope mainly. The chance for an unknown to bang suddenly famous on the mighty door of literature; the chance to be granted admission.

EVERY DAY IN THIS COUNTRY, children and adults alike are being affirmed by winning something. They're jumping up, fists thrust in the air, and screaming, "Yes!" They're falling to their knees, popping champagne corks, and smiling for the cameras. They're winning school races and district cups, their dogs and cats are winning blue ribbons, their barbecued ribs are scoring honourable mentions, and their stories are winning how-to-write books. Singers, dancers, makers of pickles, muffins, and pies—everyone's after the big win. It's not surprising that the business of selling ribbons and trophies has become a growth industry. People are making a killing by supplying these things to a public rabid for personal recognition.

Banished are the days of the singular few when the only trophies around were decades old and on display behind glass in school corridors. Now everyone's a winner. There's a generation of people who don't know the meaning of the word "last."

A FORMER HOBBY of mine was picking up used trophies at thrift stores and garage sales. It started in 1983, around the time I discovered irony, so it was an ironic hobby; it gave me an anthropological charge to discover what I thought of as an untapped vein of human banality. It was like collecting early plastic fruit or ashtrays from the fifties and sixties, something I have also done.

I have a second-place bowling trophy from "City League, 1987," and a trophy with the engraving—"Awarded To Rob—Best Husband." I've collected prize ribbons, too, and own a large blue and silver "Best Budgie in Show." It's displayed alongside an engraved plaque encased in a cube of glass that says, "Homemaker of the Year, 1971." Of course, one understands that the Best Budgie is now six inches under, that Rob, the Best Husband, has fled domestic bliss, either through death or demotion, and that the homemaker of 1971 is now a ninety-two-year-old knitter of afghans. That's the irony.

Not ironic—because we're still handing them out to one and all—are the "honourable mention" awards, surely the most demoralizing thing ever invented. To travel through life with the reminder that you were never quite as good as others is a defeating prospect. I live in fear of receiving another one.

The first one was bad enough. It was a copper-covered lead medallion awarded to me during the 1962 Victoria Dance Competition for what I thought was a stunning tap number performed in top hat and tails. I called the dance "Puttin' on the Ritz." I tapped and grinned and spun on my heels and caught my cane when I tossed it into the air as my finale, but a girl in a red satin military costume who tapped as if her legs were made of elastic won first prize. Second prize went to thin girl in a kilt who, after her Highland fling, did the splits. The splits! I was outraged. Since when do the splits go with Scottish dancing? If I hadn't felt humiliated I would have demanded an answer to this question from the judge then and there.

AN HONOURABLE MENTION is given as a nod of public congratulation. It means that at least one person has actually clapped for you, been amazed by you, and hopes you've never been happier. But because you didn't actually win the prize, it is also means: "Better luck next time," "Nice try."

At fifteen I understood what my honourable mention meant: "Give it up!" "Don't make us laugh!"

Much better was the teaching staff's attitude regarding Sports Day at my elementary school. I loved Sports Day because I was given the day off. "Don't even bother competing," the teachers told me. "You'll waste everyone's time."

I hated running races, and I couldn't jump high or long. Nor did I enjoy sweating or passing the stick in relay races or screaming at runners from the sidelines. What a sensible solution! And no teacher phoned home to worry over my self-esteem because I was inept at sports. No one insisted I waste the day "participating" and then give me a "participation" ribbon to confirm my boredom.

THERE ARE THOSE WHO DO WELL—win the prizes. Those who try—get the honourable mentions. And those who don't even bother. It is assumed that those in this latter group are the truly miserable among us.

Which brings me back to the business of judging that writing contest. In the end, I refused to hand out honourable mentions. I believe my decision was a benevolent one. I know established writers who won't enter a writing contest for fear of winning an honourable mention (we know who we are). Imagine having your name appear in a list beneath prize winners who are unknown *and* unpublished. How cruel, how demoralizing! At any rate, this is my thinking, and it is sound in my opinion. Living your life as a writer is difficult enough—

why run the risk of having your ever-present doubts affirmed, of inviting pity? Wouldn't it be kinder for a judge to simply look the other way, ignore the entry?

No one need know.

It would be the judge's little secret.

WE KEEP THE PARTY GOING

THAT FRIDAY NIGHT we fed the dog cookies from the table. After the chicken and avocado dinner with Nana and the girls we cracked open the package of cheap cookies called Home Blest—laughing over the name, wondering if "Blest" was a poor translation from the Chinese—and shared them with the dog. We also kept pouring the wine.

Taking a bite of the cookie Terry said, "Remember Peek Freans? Did you ever wonder what's a 'frean'?

He turned to his mother. "Do you know what a 'frean' is?"

"No," Nana said, "but I remember the accident."

"Oh, boy," Anna sighed, and we dampened down. We never knew when Nana would strike with the accident story, one of the recurrent themes of her visit; it was like a practical joke in reverse, the room suddenly filling with skeletons instead of pink flamingoes. During the five weeks she'd been with us we'd heard the story twenty, maybe thirty times, coming, as it did, out of nowhere like a flash fire of distress.

I was eight years old, Anna mouthed offside.

"I was eight years old," Nana began like a school recitation. "I got out of bed in the middle of the night because I heard my cat crying. And went to the top of the stairs and called her. It was pitch dark. I must have tripped on my nightgown because I fell down the stairs and hit my head on a large metal trunk that my mother kept there, at the side. I cracked open my skull. The man next door heard my screams and called an ambulance. There was blood everywhere. They had to shave my head to operate, to put my skull back together. This was in Toronto, in 1920. No one thought I'd live. The newspapers carried the story. After the operation I was taken to a lecture hall. The doctor who operated on me wanted to show his students. So everyone came and touched the hole in my forehead, the part they could only cover with skin. An operation of this kind had never been done before and the doctor was famous. He used to give me five dollars every time I was put on display."

Like P.T. Barnum, I thought. Gothic, like the nineteenth century. "Weren't you embarrassed being on stage like that?" I asked. Being on stage was a new twist.

"Hell, no," Nana said, snapping back to us, eyes wide. "A buck's a buck. And I had nothing. We were poor."

We looked again at the hole in her skull, no different to us by now than any other body part. The skin that covered it pulsated gently like a tiny lung. When she was younger her hair had covered the wound. But with age her hair had thinned and the pulsating hole was always in view. People stared; it wasn't just children.

AFTER THIS STORY Terry did his imitation jazz pianist riff to amuse her, to lighten things up, playing the air above the table where we were drinking the wine, picking over the stale cookies. "I'm the ventriloquist and the dummy at the same time!" he said, trilling away, lost in his performance.

Nana said, "You know, I'm enjoying just sitting here. And I'll leave it at that. Is this wine I'm drinking?"

"No," Terry cracked. "Hemlock."

"What a kidder," Nana said. "But he always was a pain in the neck. Growing up, they all were. Four kids. I had no choice. I was required to love them."

"*Required to love them...*" Anna repeated quietly, shocked.

Kristy leapt up from the table. "The music's too slow," she declared, and put on the new St. Germain CD, *Boulevard*. The vibes, the xylophone, the drums.

Nana said, " Drums. Drums. Drums. I've never liked a parade. People marching off. To war, usually, or remembering war like Remembrance Day. Poor old vets marching in the rain. They always make me cry. And where does a parade end up? At dying that's where."

"Dying?" Kristy asked.

"That's right," Nana said. "Dying. What's at the end of every story."

"Don't say that." This was Anna, annoyed. "Never, never say that."

"And another thing," Nana continued, ignoring her. "If my feet are cold I can't get to sleep. For that reason I go around in bare feet. The last thing I want to be is asleep. At ninety years of age my next sleep may be my last. Pour me some more of that wine."

"At ninety years of age sleeping is definitely high-risk behaviour," said her son.

"You betcha. And another thing I don't want is a weather report. I like to figure things out for myself. I don't need anyone to tell me it's raining."

"Look," Terry said, pointing at the darkened window. "It's raining!"

"What did I tell you? A smart ass."

The phone rang.

"If that's for me," Nana said, "tell them I'm not here."

BESIDES THE ACCIDENT, the black cloud was the other theme of Nana's visit. She kept going on about the black cloud she'd seen when she'd first arrived. "I've never seen a cloud so black. It just hung there outside the window. Black as the ace of spades."

"You sure it wasn't the night you were looking at?" someone asked, one of the girls.

But Nana was insistent. "No. It was a cloud. A huge black cloud. I've never seen anything like it. It was the blackest cloud I've ever seen. Like a black curtain drawn halfway down the sky. The entire length of the sky."

It was tempting to verge into metaphor. I thought of a poem: *The darkness on the horizon/ You can see it clearly now...* But stopped.

Because Nana is not a woman who thinks in metaphors. She saw a black cloud; it made an impression. That's all there was to it.

"It was the blackest cloud," she repeated. "So black. You can't imagine a blacker cloud anywhere."

Terry bent over and picked up a ball of black cat hair from the carpet. "Did it look like this?" Holding the cat hair between thumb and forefinger. "Did the cloud look like this?"

"Don't be stupid," Nana said. "That's not a cloud. When I saw *that* I thought it was a spider." She shuddered. "A spider without legs."

He pretended to put the ball of fur into his mouth. Then, imitating a magician, reached over to Nana. "What's in your mouth?" he said. "Open wide." And she did. Then put his fingers inside his mother's mouth. Out popped the ball of fur. Amazing! Everyone laughed and the candles flickered from all that hot, escaping, laughing air. Meanwhile some kind of saxophone from the CD player carried on like it owned the place. And after a while it did. So everyone shut up and listened. We became mesmerized by the music, by the ability of jazz to swing greased and unhinged, moment to moment.

"That music," Terry said, finally. "It's so fluid. The way we'd like to live our lives. Just cruising along, grooving. Even through the bad stuff that comes by the bucket load. Why is that? Why does bad stuff always come in bunches?"

"More like squalls," I said. "Storms. One damned thing after another. The leaking roof the same day the water pump goes on the car the same day your brother has a hernia operation."

"The same day the dog gets an abscess," Kristy said.

We looked at the dog, at the bandage on her paw, at her whitened old-age face.

"She's eighty-seven and a half in dog years," Anna said. "Almost as old as you, Nana."

"Poor old thing," Nana said, and the dog struggled up, wagging her tail. A Home Blest cookie was given, then another. Crumbs on the carpet, a negligible worry.

"To Mutz," I said, raising my glass.

"I'll drink to that," Nana said, and then noticed her glass was empty. "What did you do with that bottle of wine?"

We'd hidden it behind the centrepiece, a vase of hothouse tulips.

"You're cut off," Terry said, drawing a line across his throat.

"How come? The party's just begun. How can I make a toast without a drink?" He poured Nana a portion from his own glass. "Is that it?" she asked.

"For now," he said.

"You couldn't get a bird drunk on that," Nana grumbled.

The girls giggled and gave Nana the thumbs-up sign.

"The object isn't to get drunk," Terry said. "The object is to have a mellow time."

"Listen to him. Since when did he get to be in charge around here?"

"Since about thirty years ago," he said, and changed the subject. "I'll tell you how a plane flies."

"Whoopee," Nana said.

"Air weighs 14.2 pounds per square inch. Flying is all in the wings. Negative and positive pressure. A plane doesn't fly unaided. Think of it. All of us moving through weighted air. That's why spacemen float."

Off to the side Anna did a sign language imitation, flicking her arms and fingers, interpreting the inexplicable for us, like the small signing woman at the foot of the TV screen. If we were deaf we'd be deeply confused.

Finally Nana said, "You talk too much. You worry me to death."

"I'm not talking, I'm *interpreting*," Anna said.

"Well stop it," Nana said, "You're giving me a headache. That music is giving me a headache."

"Wasn't there a song that goes, 'You talk too much, you worry me to death?'" I asked.

"What I want to know," Terry said, "is who was that Italian guy that played in that big movie?"

"*Life is Fabulous? Beautiful?* A mind blow? " I said. "Roberto something."

"He surfed people's backs when he got the Oscar," Kristy said.

"Yeah. He was good. He's good."

"Here it is," Nana said, reaching for the hidden bottle and pouring herself a full glass. "To life. Down the hatch."

We watched her. I thought: Why not? What difference does it make? Take a pick:

Die at the party.

Die at the hospital or the home.

Either way the story ends.

EVERYONE AGREED it was a shame about Nana's memory. More than a shame—it was scary. Because by next morning she would have forgotten the fun she'd had the night before. And what's the point, we reasoned, of living in the moment if you forgot that moment soon after it happened? This was something we hadn't found an answer to yet.

Nana's memory—or lack of it—was evident when she drank sherry. After each glass she'd be amazed. "This is really nice!" she'd say, as if she'd never tasted sherry before. It was like that joke about the goldfish with its tiny short-term memory that kept circling its decorated bowl exclaiming, "Oh, what a lovely castle!" Then seconds later, "Oh, what a lovely castle!"

We said that to one another a lot during those five weeks.

By the end of her visit Nana was averaging four glasses of sherry a night. Worried, I measured the amount; it came to eight ounces.

"Eight ounces," I told Terry. "Are we aiding and abetting?" It was his mother, his call.

"What does it matter?" he said. "She's enjoying herself. Think: nursing home. Think: lukewarm tea in a nursing home. Where's the joy in that?"

So we gave her wine and sherry because when she drank it, somehow, miraculously, she was returned to us—if only briefly. It was a kind of testament to the benefits of alcohol; I pictured it shaking everything up in her brain, blowing the dust off synapses, kick-starting vital organs. Because Nana's former self, the person who kept up with the jokes and laughed easily, who was bright and interested and had things to say that mattered, was returned to us and it was like a gift. And because the rest of the time...

WHEN TERRY'S SISTER, Leslie, delivered her to us from Toronto, Nana was in the door first thing. "It's so good to be home," she said.

"You're not home," Leslie said, heaving the bags up the steps, exhausted. "You live in Calgary. With Norman and Jo-Anne. You've been visiting me and now you're going to visit Terry and Marion."

To us she said, "I have to keep repeating it."

To her mother: "Remember? Calgary. You forget things. You haven't lived here for two years."

Nana blinked and looked stunned. "Okay, Missy. Whatever you say."

"Comes with manual," Leslie cracked, unbuttoning her mother's coat.

PARTWAY THROUGH NANA'S VISIT we took her to a curry dinner at a friend's house. The day after it was: "Curry dinner? Don't remember it. I wasn't there."

But at the dinner, to anyone who paid attention, and they all paid some kind of attention, she said, "I'm ninety years old. I've seen a thing or two."

One of the guests was Peter, whose wife Tony is a Navajo Indian, and so has been around Native Indians and their ways. He was transfixed by Nana, by being, he said, in the presence of an elder. "You're the repository of probably two hundred years of memory," he exclaimed. "You remember stories your grandparents told."

"I had no grandparents," Nana said, sullenly. "There was just Mum and me." You could picture her in a 1920s schoolyard, chin thrust forward, defiant.

"What was your mother's name?"

"Connacher."

Jane, who was giving the dinner, laughed. "Down here at this end of the table it's the Lennens, the Kelleys, and the Fitzgeralds. Little Ireland holding down this end of the table."

Nana smiled at the mention of Ireland. "My mother came over on the boat when she was eighteen. My father was waiting for her in Toronto. They got married. Then he was killed in the war. I was six years old."

"The war?" Peter asked.

"The First World War." Nana said.

"Wow!" Peter said, but we could tell he was disappointed that her memory—the long-term memory, the one that still worked—only extended to just under one hundred years.

Still, Nana was pleased, sitting at the table with everyone, a glass of wine at hand. That would be the terrible thing about being in a nursing home, we'd decided: no adult parties, no wine and stories and easy laughter around a table. Which is why there was Nana's road trip—a few months in Toronto, a home base in Calgary, a while again with us because she'd already lived here for seventeen years and we'd done our time. But for how much longer could everyone keep this up?

Later at the curry dinner—it was after 10—Nana's jokey,

paranoid questions began. "I just want to ask one thing if you don't mind." And everyone hushed for wisdom. "I just want to know where I'm sleeping tonight." There was an uncomfortable shifting at the table.

"With us," Terry said gently. "You're staying with us. You'll go home with us."

A few minutes later she asked it again.

Then Peter suddenly stood up and filled Nana's glass and made a toast. "To the elder amongst us!"

"I'll drink to that," Nana said. "But let me tell you one more thing. I never expected to be this old."

AT THE END OF FIVE WEEKS Norman and Jo-Anne arrived from Calgary. "Like rescuing troops," they told us. They were here to take Nana home with them. I thought I'd make a special dinner. Norman and Jo-Anne were due on a 9 o'clock flight so there was just the three of us, the girls being out.

But I was rushed that day so threw together a meal of baked ham and fish, mashed potatoes, steamed vegetables. We lit candles and poured wine. But there was a sad feel to the dinner—at least for Terry and me—as though this might be a "last supper."

Then, as we began eating, I looked down at my plate and was dismayed by what a boring meal I'd served. It was like one of those remembered meals from my childhood and I was ashamed that there was nothing special about it, that I hadn't taken enough time or care.

We ate in silence, Terry and Nana chewing steadily through the pressed ham, me picking at the sole and limp broccoli. Then I said, "I'm sorry. It's a boring dinner."

"So what?" Nana said.

"But it's boring. And tasteless. It's like something from

the fifties."

"So what?" she repeated. "It'll smarten them up for the next round. They won't take things for granted."

Ella Fitzgerald was singing in the background: "*It was just one of those things. Just one of those crazy flings. A trip to the moon on gossamer wings…*"

We could see the fireplace from the table and the three cats lying on the couches, the dog sprawled, twitching in sleep. Outside the wind blew a cold December rain against the windows.

Our not-so-little version of paradise, I thought. Home.

"Unfortunately—or fortunately," I remarked, "the over-riding concern of my adult life hasn't been writing books or championing causes. It's been in *making home*. Because to be domestic, fully domestic, you must give most of your time to maintenance. The fire burns and burns because of this."

"Keeping the home fires burning," Terry snorted. "Sounds like a sentimental song from World War 2."

Nana and I liked the sentiment and ignored him.

"That's all I ever wanted," Nana said matter-of-factly. "A home. A girl and a boy, though I got two of each. And you know what? They turned into four nice people. I've got nothing to be ashamed of."

"That counts for a lot," I said.

"That counts for everything," Nana said.

NOTES ON THE WEDDING

DANIEL, THE BRIDE'S FATHER, has given our son Bill a purple polyester shirt with a ruffle down the front. Daniel was married in this shirt in the early seventies, as Bill will now be in a curious reversal of the heirloom gown. Man to man, a purple polyester shirt travels through the generations.

In their wedding pictures Daniel looks like Rick Danko from The Band; his bride, Pam, like Marianne Faithfull. There's a cloud of smoke off to the left of their grinning faces.

Even though it is now 2004, Bill says, "Far out!" when Daniel gives him the purple shirt.

"Far out" is an expression from the sixties and seventies meaning that some person, place, or thing is unbelievably good. Bill also uses the word "groovy" from those times to denote something that is not as good as "far out" but, nonetheless, all right. Bill is being ironic when he uses these terms.

MY HUSBAND SAYS, "FAR OUT" when he hears about the purple shirt, but he's using the term sarcastically. What he actually means is that he is "bummed out"—feeling disappointed—that Bill is not getting married in *his* leather suit, the one he was married in to Wife #1.

I tell him Bill claimed the outfit years ago and no one knows where it is today. Actually I am glad the dreadful thing is out of the house, what with the buckskin cowboy look, the codpiece, and the scent of Wife #1 all over it with her going-to-my-wedding-in-a-horse-and-buggy theme. Good riddance to the leather suit is what I am thinking.

FOR OUR WEDDING my husband wore grey flannel pants and a navy blue blazer, an aggressively conservative outfit. To match him I wore a blue linen suit. We looked like an accountant and a commissionaire. The suit was "something new," as was our "cop-out" in succumbing to the "Establishment," meaning the pressure from our parents now that we were parents ourselves. This was 1978 and my theme was going-to-my-wedding-in-a-nursing-bra.

RICKEY, MY HUSBAND'S BROTHER, showed up on the morning of our wedding wearing greasy bell-bottoms and a tie-dyed sweatshirt. After he used the shower and blow-dried his beard and long hair, he put on the leather suit for his transformation into best man. He looked like Dennis Hopper in *Easy Rider*.

His wedding gift to us was a bag of "grass," that is, cannabis, not garden refuse.

In the pictures everyone except my father is grinning wildly.

FOR WEDDING #1 I'd worn a knee-length cape, black tights, and Jesus sandals that laced to my knees. I'd met the man at a human be-in two weeks earlier and married him because we thought it would be a "trip"—as in, a heavy cosmic experience. Plus he slapped his forehead when he got frustrated, which was often. I was nineteen years old and found this gesture cute.

IF I WERE ALLOWED to give advice I would tell Faye, Bill's intended: Don't wear Jesus sandals and a cape to your wedding—it's *bad karma*.

Other than the purple shirt we have no idea what both will wear when they marry, but we understand that they are "doing their own thing" and so respectfully do not meddle.

AS IT STANDS, no one is invited to their wedding. This is because they're getting married in Greece—alone. They've bought a wedding package that includes a civil servant, an interpreter, two witnesses, a hotel room, dinner with champagne, the paperwork taken care of, and a donkey covered with flowers.

They are keeping quiet about the exact date of the wedding saying only that they will call both sets of parents when the deed is done, some time in June or July. We do know, however, that the island is Hydra, an island without cars, and the location of Leonard Cohen's house, the one he bought in the sixties with a bequest from his grandmother.

FOR OUR HONEYMOON my husband and I went home and fed the baby, a.k.a. the "love child." This is something we continued doing until three years ago when the love child—Bill—moved out.

BEFORE GREECE, Bill and Faye plan to attend a soccer game in Portugal. They've had tickets for a year.

"A European Cup game!" Bill exclaims. "Whoa!"

"Whoa" is a recent term meaning "far out." He is being sincere, not ironic, when he says "Whoa!"

Bill and Faye are now twenty-six years old and have advanced university degrees in anthropology and sociology, respectively.

THE NAME BILL, by the way, is a "counter culture" name, meaning it is non-conforming alongside the names people were giving their babies in 1978: Jeremy, Jason, Matthew, Ryan, Sean. We tell this to people at parties.

It's become clear, though, that "blowing minds"—shocking people—isn't what it used to be. Lately, we've been asked, "What's counter culture? Some 'flower power' thing from the sixties?"

AFTER THE GREEK WEDDING, Bill and Faye will be travelling in Europe for six weeks. They're well organized, have reservations in decent hotels, have purchased additional health-care coverage, and will be carrying valid VISA cards, vials of Ativan, cell phones.

My husband and I, on our separate trips to Europe, hitchhiked and slept on floors. Red wine cost ten cents a bottle in Spain then; you carried your matchbox full of grass in a leather pouch hidden somewhere on your body, often next to your "God's eye"—an amulet made of wool and sticks— and your bamboo flute.

AT HOME, on August 7th, Bill and Faye will have a reception at the Polish Hall in Victoria, a place large enough to accommodate two hundred people and three bands. Apart from the fifty bottles of wine that Faye's parents are providing, it will be a potluck and BYOB affair.

The Polish Hall has accommodated wedding receptions for over fifty years. There are plastic rosettes stuck permanently to the walls, round tables covered with white cloths, a stage, an area for dancing. You can almost see the ghosts of sweaty children with their best clothes askew, chasing one another during the after-dinner speeches, the drunken uncle passed out on one arm across a table strewn with empty plates and wine bottles, a conga line of middle-aged boozy women.

Of the two hundred invited guests, approximately one hundred and sixty will be under the age of thirty. They will "party hearty," a new term meaning that they will dance, get drunk, and scream. The remainder of the guests will be geriatric—parents, older relatives, family friends. These few, I worry, will be "expanding their consciousnesses"—gaining insight into the ways of the world—in the back kitchen. They'll be doing this by not getting "strung out"—fretting—over the meager size of the potluck offerings, the many bags of nacho chips, for example, brought by the young who have not understood that "potluck" means casseroles and/or salad.

AS THE WEDDING PREPARATIONS ADVANCE, word has gotten out that I was upset—"freaked out"—about not receiving an itinerary of the trip to Europe. Faye's parents received one. We did not. I assumed that several years of Insight Meditation had rendered me immune to incoming turmoil. Apparently not. My

reaction—received as "tart"—must have belied what I
thought of as serenity. Instantly, a woman who in her heart
still wears flowers in her hair becomes the slighted, frumpy
mother of the groom in all those wedding movies, the one
wearing furs and stout shoes—in other words, my grandmother.

EARLY ON Faye announces: "There's no way I'm going to be
walked down the aisle by a man and given to another man
like a commodity."

"I totally agree," I say.

"Totally" is a word favoured by the current young; my
using it means that I am completely in agreement with her,
and also that I am hip enough to speak this word although I
run the risk of being regarded as "a flake"—pathetic—by
doing so.

"We lived together four years before we got married." I
mention this fact as an alternative.

"Just like us," Faye says to Bill. "Isn't that sweet?"

"Yeah, my parents are cool."

"Cool" is a far out approval rating.

THREE MONTHS before the wedding Daniel and Pam visit and put
their family's misfits on the table.

Everyone understands that families marry one another.

A crazy aunt is mentioned, a paranoid grandfather. We in
turn divulge a schizophrenic cousin, several drunks, an in-
clination to hypochondria, and Bill's Uncle Rickey, who, in
these egalitarian times, is not called an old hippie but a "free-
spirited alternative" even though he now runs a bar and
marina.

And while we are no longer "beautiful people" and have left our "matchboxes" far behind, we assure Daniel and Pam that we have retained some of the values from former times. To this end, we mention that Bill has been raised on whole grains, organic fruits and vegetables, vitamin supplements and supervised TV.

Later we wonder if Daniel and Pam, in spite of their wedding pictures, were "heads" or "straight" back then, a coin toss meaning wanderers on the astral plane or uptight members of "The System." They're grey haired now, like us, own their own home, and drive a Toyota.

"Hard call," my husband says.

BILL AND FAYE have asked us to make the party invitations.

"Because you're so good at making cards," Bill smoothly adds.

He's thinking of a Christmas card we made called "Kristmas Kraft" with instructions on how to make a Kraft nativity scene: "*First hollow out a three pound brick of your favourite luncheon meat so that it resembles a stable and so that you, looking down through its roof, look like an angel…*"

"We don't want anything cheesy," Bill has instructed. "No bells or birds or fog or cakes. And nothing that says: 'Two Lives. One Path.' We got one of those and threw up."

They want a party invitation that is ironic—unique and hilarious. A card that is not clichéd, or, if it is, ironically clichéd.

We select three possible images for their consideration: red and beige graphics from a matchbook—a rooster and a hen above a caption that reads "Best Match;" a drunken scene from an Hieronymus Bosch painting; and the Roy Lichtenstein comic book painting *In the Car*—a blonde woman in a leopard skin coat, a darkly handsome man driving. Bill and Faye reject the "Best Match" image because no one will get the joke. It would look too cute, they say, and anything cute must be avoided. They liked the other choices, though, and have picked them both.

OUR PARENTS OF THE GROOM outfits for the Polish Hall party are hanging in the closet. I'm going as a Greek matron in a black dress and shawl. My husband is wearing a white, short-sleeved, over-the-pants shirt with blue and yellow embroidery down the front. When he takes the shirt into the bike repair shop to show his friend, the owner, the tattooed kid who works there gasps, "Dope shirt, man. Rad!"

A DIGITAL CAMERA will be one of our wedding gifts to Bill and Faye, along with the Polish Hall rental and a donation towards the trip. The camera purchase does not go smoothly.

After we finally settle on a particular store and model, a camera is bought. Later my husband consults the internet and discovers that our camera choice was not a good buy. He returns it, unopened, the next day, intending to exchange it for a model that costs twenty dollars more.

The salesman is incredulous. "You mean you didn't even try it out?"

"That's right."

"You mean you believe those reviews on the internet?"

"Right again."

"Any idiot knows those reports aren't reliable! One bad review and just like that it's all over the world!"

"Look, I just want to exchange the camera. And who are you calling an idiot?"

This goes on for half an hour. The manager is called in.

The salesman says, "I can't believe you didn't even try the camera."

My husband says, "Look, forget about that. I don't want to try the freaking camera. I want that one there, on the shelf."

The manager says, "Now, now, no need to get excited."

"Who's excited? I just want—"

The manager says, "Just take the camera home and try it out. See for yourself."

"No."

The salesman, a pudgy, red-headed guy about fifty, says through clenched teeth: "Let me put it this way. I know about cameras and you don't. Everyone has an expertise. Mine is cameras."

And my husband, who's spent most of his working life in the school system dealing with the "problem cases," says loudly, "Well, I have an expertise, too. And mine's dealing with assholes."

In this instance, an asshole is a jerk.

My husband gets the camera he wants.

THE WEDDING PLANS expand when Bill and Faye announce that they've bought a Canadian marriage license because they've decided to get married in a civil ceremony here before the Greek wedding.

"It would cost six hundred dollars to get the paperwork done between the two countries," Faye tells us.

She also says she's heard from a friend that in Greece it takes five to ten years to get a divorce, which is practical thinking on her part. Really, quite adult.

Being that adult about my wedding would never have occurred to me—either time.

They want a significant date for their Canadian marriage and have chosen June 1st because that is Bill's grandparents' wedding anniversary.

On that day a marriage commissionaire is going to their house. The only people invited are their best friends, who will act as witnesses.

Once again, they are "doing their own thing" while we, in response are acting "laid back" because we don't want to send any "bad vibes"—negative feelings—their way.

We do send a dozen yellow roses, though, timed to arrive before the ceremony.

Afterwards, Bill phones to say the deed is done.

"What did Faye wear?" I ask after the congratulations.

"A black top. Some skirt."

"And you?"

"The purple shirt. Jeans."

Faye gets on the phone and tells us that she would like their Greek wedding to occur on Canada Day, July 1st, so that whenever she hears fireworks she'll be reminded of her second wedding day.

We tell her this is a brilliant idea. Get the first marriage over with quickly, as we did. Move onto the second one, the one with the fireworks.

WE OPEN A BOTTLE of champagne and phone Daniel and Pam. They're also drinking champagne. We talk on four phones.

"Mind blowing, isn't it?" my husband says. "To think that once they were babies."

"Yeah," Daniel says. "Outtasight." He sounds flat.

Later we wonder if Daniel is being ironic when he uses the term "outtasight." Or whether, like us, he is feeling "down," as in left out, a little sad, old.

THREE INTRUSIONS

A BILLBOARD ON THE HIGHWAY into town had the word "vagina" written on it in twelve-foot-tall letters. The large red word was set against a plain white background and covered the entire billboard; below the word was some hard-to-read smaller print. At first I didn't know what the word was supposed to mean. It was confusing to see a billboard like this amongst the usual harmless ones—*Stop the Seal Hunt!*, *Visit Butchart's Gardens, Holiday for Less at Accent Motels*. Maybe it's a misogynist's slur, I thought. Or the name of a new garden centre, or real estate agent. No doubt lots of people driving by, like me, wondered what the connection was. Some, probably, had to have the word explained to them, that it actually did not refer per se to "the sheath-like covering of the sexual passage in the female body leading from the uterus to the external orifice" (OED), but something else.

A revived play, as it turned out. One in which the public was invited to celebrate vaginas, have panel discussions about them, and even to laugh about the way vaginas could talk to one another. There was a lot of discussion about the play on radio and TV talk shows that fall, and in newspapers and magazines.

In any case, the giant-size word on the billboard made me think of vaginas *in general* and that, in turn, made me think of William Burroughs. The play was encouraging us to have meaningful conversations with vaginas in the same way, it seemed, that William Burroughs so famously had conversations with his talking asshole. Which apparently cracked jokes, held opinions, and eventually ate him. A fitting end to the man, some might say, but not, I think, the end the vagina play had in mind.

Still, I wondered. What if, instead of the author of the play, horror writer Stephen King had got hold of the idea of talking vaginas? I thought of him because of what he'd said in a *Paris Review* interview I'd recently read. That in his books what you see is an observation of ordinary middle-class North American life and what happens "when people have to deal with something inexplicable." In other words, when the extraordinary intrudes into ordinary life. The billboard with its enormous word and the shock value it garnered was a good example of such an intrusion.

In his novels, Stephen King is always asking "What if?" Seeing the same billboard I saw, I wondered if he might then say: "What if middle-class citizens were suddenly faced with not only scores of talking vaginas but with vaginas which were also marauding and hungry? What would happen next?"

This "What if" formula is the bedrock of Stephen King's storytelling. He used it in *Pet Cemetery*—What if dead pets ate children? In *Carrie*—What if a bullied high school girl had the gift of telekinesis? In *Cujo*—What if a marauding rabid dog bit people and caused them to become marauding rabid people?

Writer and cartoonist James Thurber had no need of the "What if?" question. He addressed the idea of devouring vaginas, you might say, head on. A well-known cartoon of his has a puny, bald husband standing beside his marriage bed wearing mismatched pyjamas while his gorgon of a wife—she's twice his size—is sitting up in bed on one elbow and scowling at him. *Well, it matters to me!* says the caption.

Actually, most of Thurber's cartoons are about devouring vaginas—about the bullying, fun-sapping female. Apparently this was a basic fear of Thurber's, and scores of his contemporaries. In fact, his stories and cartoons still resonate with people—both male and female. As does a certain play about talking vaginas.

THE SECOND INTRUSION into ordinary life occurred not long after the billboard incident, via an email chain letter. The first sentence read, "This is a panty exchange!" The woman who sent the email was unknown to me, but I knew one of the other recipients vaguely. What can this mean? I wondered. And why does a stranger want to exchange underpants with me?

I read on. "Send one pair of *new* panties—with the tag attached—to the person at the top of the list and then add your name to the bottom. Within weeks," the letter promised, "you will receive thirty-six pairs of panties in the mail. Thirty-six pairs for the price of one!"

I was not going to cooperate with this chain letter because I hate the word panties. Panties, in my opinion, are worn by dimwits and squealers. Intelligent women wear underpants—sturdy, practical, sequestered. Panties are bits of fluff that hang themselves from lampshades like cobwebs. Underpants are modest and deep-thinking; their wearers read *Freedom and Dread* by Søren Kierkegaard to unwind.

Besides, owning thirty-six pairs of underpants is extravagant; that's a lot of underpants to keep track of. It works out to five weeks' worth, if you wear a new one every day. The ones I received during my childhood with the days of the week emblazoned on the bum—red for Saturday, white, of course, for Sunday, and so on—took enough time to sort out.

In any case, the email letter instructed me to shop for a large-sized pair of panties for the stranger at the top of the list—Cynthia. Beside Cynthia's name was the shy request— "no thongs, please." I was then told to duplicate the letter and send six copies to my friends. Friends who, upon receiving it, would cease to be my friends. But this, of course, is why you send chain letters to people you barely know—there is no friendship there to be lost.

"We can all use some fun and crazy panties!" the letter said, continuing the pitch. I hadn't thought about that. Would receiving thirty-six pairs through the mail make me a fun and crazy person? I've occasionally had hopes in that direction, but there was no guarantee. And how, exactly, would this be accomplished? By panting to the mailbox and ripping apart the panty packages? By squealing over colour and style? By thinking of nothing else for days on end? That might be an escape; I'll give it that. No more pondering over life's many lack of meanings.

Like any chain letter, this one carried a warning about non-compliance. "Seldom does anyone drop out," the letter said in closing. Death was not mentioned, which was surprising because death is the usual threat for non-compliance in chain letters, if not your own physical death, then the death of your hopes and dreams.

I was quick to reply to the sender: "So sorry, can't manage.

Have tons of underpants already. But thanks for asking."
This last bit because you can never be too careful.

SHORTLY AFTER THE PANTY EMAIL, an April issue of a woman's magazine provided me with the third example of intrusion into
ordinary life. The magazine was an impulse buy at the check-
out counter at Sidney Super Foods. I was taken with the
cover—pink with yellow roses—which managed to appear
both psychedelic and homey. And with the headlines: *203
Bright Spring Ideas! Streamline Your Wardrobe! Delicious
Off-the-Shelf Meals!* I'll flip through this later, I thought,
after I've unpacked the groceries. I'll read it with a cup of
tea, and looked forward to a peaceful half hour with my
feet up.

When I finally got to the magazine it didn't disappoint. I
enjoyed the usual makeover articles, recipes, spring fashions,
and decorating ideas. But a column in the "Ask the Experts"
section gave me a jolt because it was so unexpected. Alongside advice from a financial planner, a nutritionist, and a fit-
ness instructor, was advice from a certified sex therapist on
how to give a man a hand job.

My god! I thought. Is this what Canadian women are
getting up to in their homemaking magazines? Is this what all
that "domestic science" I learned in high school Home Ec
classes has come to? I read the column avidly.

The how-to instructions, it was soon clear, were going to
be no-nonsense, like a visit to the hardware store. Where I
might have hoped for descriptive flourishes, or, at the very
least, adjectives or exciting verbs, the column instead provided a "Five-Step Procedure." Before we got to that, though,
a few sentences were mentioned about the proper way to
hold a penis, as if a penis were a power saw or an electric

drill, something completely foreign to a woman. "Always remember to use a gentle rotating movement," the columnist said, "and remember to stroke the testicles."

"Write that down, class," as my Home Ec teacher, Miss Horrel, might have said. "It'll be on the test."

Next, the "The Five-Step Procedure" was presented. I found it confusing. Diagrams would have been helpful; I always like a picture with a recipe. So I can see how things might turn out if I'm diligent and follow instructions, don't skimp on ingredients or skip steps as I'm liable to do. But there were no diagrams to accompany the "The Five-Step Procedure."

The columnist did mention, though, that she was calling the procedure "Ode to Bryan" after the friend who had shared it with her. I thought this was very public-spirited of Bryan and would have loved to have seen a picture of him. I imagined him to be a shy man, perhaps a postal worker or a government clerk in the Department of Vital Statistics. He'd be in his forties, single, a little on the plump side, and with a receding hairline, and a few endearing freckles sprinkled across the bridge of his nose. Failing a picture of Bryan, a picture of his penis would have been helpful, together with the practitioner's hand position. *Like This!* The caption would say. Arrows would point to the significant area and there would be medical terms to give the column clinical authenticity.

After Step One—"Apply lubricant, oil, or a silicone-based product, but make sure to warm it in the palm of your hand first"—the Five-Step Procedure bogged down. Step Two was baffling. "Sit between your partner's legs." I got that okay. But the next part of Step Two was to "place the palm of your hand on your partner's penis so that your elbow is out at a 90-degree angle." This is where they lost me, especially when instructed to "wrap your thumb around the penis so that your wrist pushes on your partner's stomach." That didn't sound right to me. It sounded like a recipe for making your partner projectile vomit. All that single-mindedly pushing on his stomach could only result in the wrong kind of eruption. Steps 3 through 5 were mainly about "rotating the glans" and "maintaining First Position" (elbow at the crucial 90-degree angle), and about the importance of changing hands, for rest's sake, this last point a considerate, though tossed-off, touch by the columnist, I felt. Too little, too late.

Throughout, no mention was made about how long the Five-Step Procedure would take. About the pros and cons of being naked while performing the procedure, or about the importance of mood, lighting, music, drink, and/or sleeping children. What was stressed was that the Five-Step Procedure was a good strategy for a woman to use when she can't have sex, such as during her period, or if she has a yeast infection. I took particular note of the term "can't have" as opposed to, say, "Buzz off, darling, I'm busy." The columnist didn't mention the times when a woman would rather, for example, read, floss her teeth, de-flea the dog, or compose an ode to Larry, Curly, and Moe. Clearly, the only acceptable "excuses" for not having sex on demand were periods, or yeast infections, hence the Five-Step Procedure, designed to help a woman negotiate through this difficult time.

But maybe I nitpick. What better way to handle a pesky household chore than with a Five-Step Procedure, something practical to have on hand when duty calls? For some—male and female—it was, no doubt, useful information. The column could be cut out, tacked to the fridge, kept in the car's glovebox, carried in a pocket or purse. This quick option, like a fast off-the-shelf meal, might be a godsend to the busy homemaker, as important as duct tape or a standby case of mushroom soup.

But I don't want to forget Bryan in all of this and his service to North American women. Homemakers everywhere should give Bryan a great big hand.

LIBERATING THE PETS

OUR OLD CAT MARGARET had arthritis. Because of the damp West Coast climate we live in. It was winter and she was suffering, howling every time she moved. So we wondered how we could help her, and came up with the idea of packing her in a crate and shipping her to Scottsdale, Arizona. It seemed like a perfect solution. We figured the warmer temperatures there would do her good. She was twenty years old. We figured six months in Scottsdale, Arizona—mean temperature in the high seventies—would be just the thing for her old bones. Like a reward for being a good cat. Like a dream vacation.

We had a friend in Scottsdale, Arizona who'd said, "Drop in any time."

I asked my husband, "Do you think the invitation includes the cat?"

"Why not?" he said. "A man who signs his Christmas cards with love from him and his cats and his wife—putting the cats before the wife—would understand. He'd welcome her with open arms."

I checked it out. If Margaret had a rabies shot, and we bought a specially designed metal crate to put her in, she could travel air freight; it was surprisingly cheap. "We could make a bed for her out of one your old T-shirts," I told my husband. "Her crate will smell like home."

She likes my husband's smell the best. For twenty years she's sought out his clothes to sleep on. For twenty years he's looked like a black-tipped shag carpet, one that strides happily through the world shedding detritus.

We were serious about shipping Margaret to Arizona. After takeoff we could leave a message on our friend's answering machine: "Guess what? Our cat's paying you a surprise visit!" We laughed our heads off just thinking about it.

The man I spoke to at the airport said Ralph, the freight supervisor, would call us back to get further details.

The things we do for our animals.

When the dog turned eleven, as a birthday present, we threw out her collar and leash. "She's earned her freedom," we said. "Why not let her do what she likes *when* she likes?" This is something newly retired people say. So we retired the dog.

"It's not necessary to guard the door any more," we told Mutz, a golden retriever cross. "Take it easy! Start a hobby! These are your golden years!" She moved permanently onto our bed and has never looked back.

Because she has a bad hip we've replaced her walks with Sunday drives. "Who wants an ice cream cone?" we yell, and, deliriously happy, she limps to the door. During the drive she sits in the back seat smiling, deeply interested in every tree and car we pass. When she gets the cone—always chocolate—she licks it delicately while we hold it for her. She's become a really good senior dog, not too demanding, always grateful. This is behaviour we're keeping in mind for *our* senior years: act deliriously happy and run for the door when you're asked out; be pleasant and interested; say please and thank you; remember to wipe your mouth after you've eaten. And work on your smile; make sure it's thin and ingratiating. It's a winning combination. And if you're lucky your kids might ship you to Arizona for the warmth.

Cat and dog hair was the reason we bought a new vacuum cleaner. It had become impossible to tell the colour of our carpets. The day we thought about sending Margaret to Arizona we drove to the mall. We'd never had a new vacuum cleaner before. We'd had a succession of wrecks my mother-in-law had thrown out. So we were excited. There was a festive feel in the air. It was going on credit.

Mutz was grinning on the seat between us. When we arrived we told her, "Don't even bother growling at passersby. The car's a junker. No one wants it. And you're a matted old dog. No one wants you, either. So put up your feet, have a snooze."

Walking into the appliance department at the Bay I was glad I'd dressed up; I had on black pants and leather boots; I wore makeup and silver earrings. The occasion demanded it. I felt like a big shot with money to burn. My husband acted the same way. He was swaggering, seemed bulkier, cavalier. He was wearing one of the sports coats his brother-in-law had thrown out. There was a small branch sticking out from the lapel like a renegade boutonniere; cat and dog hair flew out from his sleeves; there was a furry nap to his jeans. He looked like a large, friendly animal. The kind you'd take to a nursing home or a hospital so the inhabitants could pet him and say, "Who's a good boy? Who's a good old thing?"

We found the vacuum section behind displays of stainless steel fridges, wall ovens, and dishwashers with see-through doors. With the help of the teenage salesclerk, we chose a sleek, top-of-the-line vacuum that was cherry red in colour. It was beautiful. It had a feature called Swivel Glide Vision, and headlights so it could see under the bed.

Once home, my husband studied the instruction manual while I unpacked the vacuum and plugged it in. The headlights flashed on, the roar was deafening. I noticed the vacuum looked even more beautiful when placed alongside our shabby furniture. Owning it gave me a charge. I couldn't get over the way I suddenly felt solid and respectable.

After vacuuming for a while I discovered the border on the living room carpet was a bright shade of red. Soon the reusable container was full of thick, gray matter that looked like slimy dust. My husband came to investigate.

"That's disgusting!" he cried. "You know what we are? We're animals!"

He looked at me accusingly. I merely answered the phone. It was my cousin Shirley. Since the kids have left home there's been a tag team of callers checking up on us. They're worried we may succumb to that feared affliction, Empty Nest syndrome, the breeding ground for madness and/or divorce amongst suddenly childless couples. How to tell them we're having a blast buying a vacuum cleaner, liberating the pets?

Moments later there was another call—from Ralph, the freight supervisor, at the airport. Ralph told me that Margaret couldn't fly to Arizona unaccompanied. "What if no one claimed her?" he asked. There was an outraged squeak to his voice. "What if she croaked en route? She's an old cat. We'd be liable. You could sue."

I told my husband. "Too bad," he said. "We could have cleaned up in the lawsuit."

We woke Margaret and told her the news. She was lying on the old blue heating pad. "Trip's off," we said. "So much for your dream vacation. You're stuck with us."

But back to the vacuum cleaner. There was no denying the way it made me feel. Its purchase convinced me that my position against acquiring material things had become as worn out as our chesterfield. Suddenly the future seemed bright; there'd be credit card applications to fill out.

"This new vacuum's going to change our lives," I told my husband. "It's a harbinger. We're going to start moving up in the world."

"How do you know?"

"Don't you see? The vacuum's an indicator of the Big Change that's coming. I can feel it in my bones. It's our first *new* purchase in years. Our ship is coming in."

"It's a vacuum cleaner."

"Yes! But because we've started with the vacuum we can move on. Change everything. The car, the thrift-store clothes, the second-hand furniture. That's been our problem. For years. We've been surrounded by crap. It'll be a new beginning."

"You sound like a politician."

"Think of it. All the old stuff gone."

"We'd be living in an empty house."

"But wouldn't that be a good thing? It'd be purifying. Spiritual, almost. Like accidental Zen."

"Give me a break."

"Remember what your mother always said," I reminded him. "'There's no sense in *looking* poor.'"

"She said that when she put on her thirty-year-old mink coat. And who's to know we have a new vacuum cleaner? Are you suggesting we put it on the front porch for the neighbours to see?"

"There's an idea!"

IT'S TWO YEARS LATER and the broken-beyond-repair new vacuum is being stored in the shed out back; one day, my husband says, he'll get around to fixing it. Meanwhile, we're still debating how to launch our ascent in the world. It's difficult to begin a new beginning, though I still believe that if you change one thing in your life for the better, other things will fall into place. Unfortunately this is still a theory because the new vacuum seized up a month after its warranty ran out. From too much responsibility in its role as a harbinger, I think.

The good news is that Margaret is still with us. She's now twenty-two years old. House cats, I've read somewhere, live between nine and seventeen years, so Margaret has already broken a record. She weighs two and a half pounds, still chirps at us, and is obsessed with food. When she's not on her heating pad, or using the litter box, she's sitting at the foot of the fridge. She's crazy about pastrami, dill pickles, marinated olives. We think she has a tapeworm. A two-and-a-half-pound tapeworm.

Still, I can't get the idea of changing our luck out of my mind. I'm thinking this might happen when Margaret, as Ralph the freight man put it, croaks. In the meantime we spoil her. A couple of weeks ago she had a lion cut to get rid of her Rasta-like mats. It was a close shave, leaving only her head, feet, and the tip of her tail covered with dull black fur. We laughed our heads off when we saw her. Then I bought her almond butter because she likes it. A small jar costs five dollars. I told my husband, "A little goes a long way. Use it sparingly, the way you would cortisone."

Margaret likes licking almond butter from his fingers. I like creating new sources of anxiety for myself. The newest one: guarding the almond butter. My husband thought that Margaret eating the almond butter from his fingers was cute until he accidentally poured half the jar over her head.

"Oh my god!" I screamed. "The waste! The waste!"

Holding onto the cat my husband reached for a teaspoon. "Give me the jar," he said. "This can be saved."

THE FLIGHT OF BROWN OWL

BROWN OWL RAN OFF with the tai chi master. Left her husband of twenty-eight years, two kids, one grandson, and ran off to Puerto Rico. A month before this happened we saw them necking in the Safeway parking lot on a busy Saturday afternoon. We thought the tai chi master must be Latin because of the way he moved, which was fluid and slow-dancing and dominant. We didn't see his face that day, just his poncho-covered back embracing Brown Owl. We got a good look at her, though. She had on a low-necked sleeveless top and her head was thrust back and between kisses she was laughing.

Fifteen years earlier Brown Owl had been our daughter's Brownies leader. That's why, until we got to know her, we always referred to her as Brown Owl. She taught Anna to sew buttons, and make a fire out of paraffin and twigs, and also the Brownie Promise, which is "I promise to do my best, to be true to myself, my God/Faith and Canada; to help other people; and to keep the Brownies Law." This law concerned being honest and taking care of the world, not a bad law to abide by.

I always thought it interesting that Lady Baden-Powell, who took over responsibility for the Brownies and Guides from her husband, the Lord, in 1918 because he wanted to involve himself exclusively with Cubs and Scouts, first named the girls Rosebuds. I can't imagine how the organization would have survived to this day if the woodsy Brownies hadn't replaced the nymph-like Rosebuds as a name early on. Brown Owl would have been called something else, something pink, and the whole slant of the organization would have taken a Lolita turn.

In any case, in 1988 Brown Owl is there in the year-end picture with Anna's troop wearing her brown clothes—dress, shoes, and cap—a plump woman looking earnestly at the camera. She'd stitched a lot of badges onto the sleeves of her dress.

She was not a militaristic Brown Owl, as some are, everything rules and procedure. She was easygoing with the girls, something I appreciated, though some mothers found her lax on discipline. And sometimes she didn't show up at the school gym for Brownies because she'd forget it was Tuesday. Tawny Owl had to take over. Tawny Owl's clothes were gray, as befits a lesser official.

As it turned out, we were wrong about the tai chi master being Latin. He was as British as an old biscuit, and named Philip. Still, he was a master. Imagine being called a master, we said, of anything. This fact, his assumed eminence that is, might have contributed to Brown Owl keeping the Brownies Promise to be true to herself and, hence, fleeing her former life. Because the tai chi master wasn't much to look at, a man in his fifties, small in stature, with thin, sandy-coloured hair and pale skin. For someone who'd dazzled us with his hot moves in the Safeway parking lot he was, most of the time, reserved. We decided that this reserve was really a British form of serenity—on account of the tai chi.

They stayed here on two occasions. Brown Owl—Melinda—was a friend of Jeff's, our tenant who lived in the downstairs suite. So we were a second-hand party to the romance and, hence, entitled to the story.

Jeff and Melinda had taken a tai chi class from Philip who was visiting from England. This is how Melinda and Philip met. They had fallen instantly, Jeff said, in love. Or, as Jeff further told us, "The dragon sighs and the tiger roars." Meaning, as he explained to our uncomprehending faces, that Melinda and Philip were a powerful yin and yang situation; their union was inevitable.

In any event, the romance went from a spark to a bonfire within days. Melinda left her husband, who had a roofing business, and began staying with Philip at the Travelodge motel on Beacon Avenue. But that got expensive, so they stayed here for three weeks in Jeff's suite, while they got organized for their flight to Puerto Rico. Jeff gave them the bedroom; he took the pullout in the suite's living room.

It was summer. The three of them practised tai chi on the back lawn. Afterwards they'd sit around the table and umbrella out front of the suite and drink herb tea. We often observed Melinda and Philip hugging. And sometimes she'd sit on his lap and he'd lean into her breasts which were fairly large and unhinged. We observed how happy she looked with her long, golden-hued hair and textile clothing. Not bad for fifty-four, we said, lovely actually, and slimmer than she had been when she was Brown Owl and had worn the brown dress with all the badges. Though a little vacant upstairs, we thought, but tai chi might have been responsible for that—all the emptying out of the mind you're supposed to do.

Melinda collected seed pods from our wisteria vines

while she was here. To dry, she said, and put into the rattles she was learning to make. An ancient art, she told us, and sacred. Often she and Philip would wander hand in hand around the garden, stopping every now and then to smell the butterfly bush, or pick a sprig of potentilla to put in each other's hair.

They were vegetarians—Melinda, Philip, and Jeff—and ate a lot of eggs that summer. We could smell the eggs frying up here where we live in the second storey of the house. They also boiled pinto beans and mashed them with green peppers and chilies, but sometimes they went out for a meal, to the new Thai restaurant in town.

Jeff had lived in the suite for five years by then. Before that my mother-in-law had lived there for seventeen years. We'd rented the suite furnished, so Jeff used my mother-in-law's towels, sheets, and some of her dishes though the bed was new. It took a while for us to get used to a different person living downstairs. We became careful of our movements and kept our music low, things we never did for my mother-in-law.

Jeff was a gentle man in his early forties who tended his elderly parents a few streets over. They paid him enough to live on so he didn't need to work. He set out bird feeders around the suite—he could identify all the song birds—and grew succulents, and, inside, orchids, often inviting us in to look at a new bloom. There was a small cement Buddha he'd placed in the flower bed beneath the suite's windows and we'd notice him now and then sitting cross-legged before it and meditating. Occasionally he had a woman down there; one we called Spanky because he told my husband she liked to be spanked. But we didn't hear any of this because the ceiling's insulated.

When we'd look out from the upstairs windows at

Melinda, Philip, and Jeff doing their tai chi moves on the back lawn, the three of them in perfect sync like a slow ballet, we'd often comment on how the birds flying past—the gulls, crows, and smaller birds—seemed to be moving with them, all of them in tune with the exact pace of the natural world. It was beautiful to watch. Doing tai chi they seemed to be languidly embracing the world. And they stepped so lightly in their bare feet. Later, when we were working in the garden after they'd gone out, we'd notice that there was little evidence in the grass of their footfalls.

MELINDA AND PHILIP left for Puerto Rico at the end of that summer. Philip had a seasonal job at a resort there offering tai chi classes to people on vacation. The former husband—Vance—then started visiting Jeff, almost weekly. The fact that Vance had a gray ponytail and a gold earring gave us hope for his recovery, that these things meant he'd be open to new possibilities, that he wouldn't stay bitter about his fleeing wife for too long. Then Jeff started teaching him tai chi and we thought that might help, as well.

Several months after Melinda and Philip had left for Puerto Rico, Jeff told us that Melinda was back because she'd been deported. Her visa had expired but she'd ignored this fact and tried to stay on anyway. She returned to our town, leaving Philip behind at his job.

There was a happy ending, though.

She house-sat in the area for a few months and then stayed here for two weeks with Jeff while she got her papers in order. Then Philip came and got her. By then it was summer again. The last time we saw her she was striding arm in arm with Philip along Beacon Avenue. It was a hot, bright afternoon in late July, the day they were scheduled to catch a late flight to Puerto Rico. She wore a green silk scarf around her neck; it flowed behind her and caught the light brilliantly. Her long, loose hair, now orange-hued, bounced on her shoulders as she walked. There was an ecstatic look on her face but whether this was caused by her finding her master or her man or both I had no way of telling.

She and Philip, we've since heard, plan to live in Puerto Rico permanently. With Melinda's divorce settlement they've bought a house there. And Vance is building himself a smaller place with his share of the money. He's cut his hair and re-moved his earring, so things are changing for him, as well.

After living for six years in our suite, Jeff found love and moved to a Gulf Island with his girlfriend Skye. She has long grey hair and moves like a twenty-year-old. She does large oil paintings of flowers, and both she and Jeff tend their newly-planted vegetable garden. They practice tai chi in their small front yard and can see the sea as they go through their motions. It's either rough, flat grey, or sparkling in the dis-tance, Jeff has since told us, depending on the weather.

Jeff left behind a large cactus for us as a parting gift. It was a cactus I had particularly admired, and not, we think, a comment on our performance as landlords. We, in turn, gave him a book and a jar of blackberry jam, the blackberries picked from the bushes that border our yard. He lit sweet grass in the suite on the day he moved out and used an eagle feather to waft the smoke through the open windows—in case, he told us, he, or Melinda, Philip, Vance, or Skye, or any of his former women friends, had left behind negative energy. His nephew, too, Jeff added. This was Nathaniel, a morose young man with Rasta hair who'd worked for weeks in our back yard creating a Mandela out of burned match sticks. Nathaniel had stayed with Jeff for a couple of months one time because his parents didn't know what to do with him.

There were others who visited Jeff, or stayed with him, over the years. One was a man named John who self-published a book condemning capitalist society. We tried to read it but couldn't make sense of it. And John scared us slightly. He had the wild eyes and frenzied manner of a deranged person, as if he was permanently plugged into an ECT machine. To our relief he moved to Mexico. He was enraged because he couldn't sell his books. He left several cases of them behind in Jeff's suite. This meant that Jeff had to take the books to the dump before he moved out.

But now the suite is empty. There are no ghosts down there because Jeff took care of that, and the rooms seem strangely static. The furniture is in place—table, chesterfield, bed—like a stage set waiting for the cast to arrive. In the meantime we play our music loud and wonder what roles the new actors will be performing, and, more to the point, if we even want to see another play.

SEND OFF

IT WAS 8:30 ON A TUESDAY MORNING. We'd parked our cars beside the crematorium and walked to the gravesite which was so near the road we could see the faces of people in cars as they sped by in rush-hour traffic. Some drank from paper cups, some talked on cell phones, a few glanced out their car windows. Perhaps they were feeling sorry for us, or glad—that it wasn't them standing around a grave. There were nineteen family members. Rain was promised.

We were an ordinary-looking group, not dressed any differently than if we'd been attending a kid's soccer game, or picking up groceries. From passing cars we wouldn't have looked tragic or noble but ordinary, like the mourners we were—dishevelled, awkward, and wearing jackets that were too bright for the occasion.

We were waiting for Gordon Thurston. This was the funeral facilitator who had been hired to perform both the ceremony at the gravesite and the one afterwards at the funeral home. Gordon Thurston was late, though the two funeral attendants were there—a thin man in a brown suit who had sharp features and sallow skin, and a plump woman in a white sweater set who wore a large crucifix around her neck and a pleated tartan skirt. They'd arrived earlier with the coffin—white—which now rested on chrome supports above the grave. The hole beneath the coffin was hidden by a bright green cover that looked like Astroturf.

No one spoke while we waited though some of us exchanged looks. The attendants, meanwhile, stood on either end of the coffin like military guards. They had their hands clasped before them, their feet a little apart; you had the sense this was a regulation stance, one listed in the *Funeral Attendants Handbook* alongside a reminder to keep one's eyes averted so as to not intrude on the family's sorrow.

We were sad, certainly, but not that sad. The woman who died—my aunt—was ninety-eight years old, a great-grandmother. Our attitude was: being so close to the age of a century, how could death be anything but expected? Wonderfully, she was healthy to the end, lived in her own home, and went, as they say, quickly. As a result most of us were feeling hopeful—lucky!—to have come from such a hearty relative.

A light rain began falling and then, dramatically, wind blew leaves from the surrounding trees. The attendants remained in place by the coffin; the woman's skirt rustled and the man's thin black hair flew up from his head. Very professional the way they're continuing to stand in the wind and rain, I thought, almost decorous, as if they were guarding a palace. Then I thought: they're attending the coffin; they're a remnant from times past when three nuns would be hired to sit with the corpse through the night; the corpse, which was not in a cooler somewhere awaiting burial, but laid out on the dining room table in their best suit or dress; the corpse who was kept company for three days before burial, during which time people would visit—neighbours, family, friends—everyone getting the full dose of death and having a get-together while eating cakes and drinking tea and Scotch in the kitchen. By comparison, our send-off was a meager one.

We waited fifteen minutes. Then a Dodge Omni drove through the cemetery gate and sped towards us. Gordon Thurston apologized for being late; it was the traffic, he said. He was maybe sixty, white-haired, and wore a white turtleneck sweater beneath a navy blue sports jacket. He smiled kindly.

The service began. He asked us to bow our heads. We tried to hear him above the traffic roar, words that were mildly biblical, about love and life: "blessed," "journey," "love," "hope," "peace" and "everlasting." Some of us cried. It was all over in five minutes.

We didn't know what to do then because we were expecting the green cloth to be removed so the coffin could be lowered. But this didn't happen. The attendants stayed where they were, looking nowhere, while Gordon Thurston explained that interment would occur later, after the service at the funeral home when the floral tributes would be placed on the grave. There was to be no tossing of last roses.

So we left and walked back to our cars. The white coffin on the green cloth remained where it was, rudely exposed and alone; from a distance it looked like a monstrous cake. She wouldn't have liked being left on display like that, I thought; she wouldn't like that we'd left her.

LATER, AT THE FUNERAL HOME, we relaxed. We could smell the coffee brewing in the adjoining social room, and the egg sandwiches we'd be having after the public service. There were close to forty people sitting in the memorial chapel waiting for that service to begin. We hurried to the front seats.

My cousins had arranged items from their mother's life on a table upfront: her teapot with its pink and blue knitted tea cozy; a pin cushion with a needle and thread; her small green watering can; a bowl of jelly beans because this was her favourite candy. Also displayed were several floral arrangements and wreaths with florist's tags attached to them stating the names of the senders.

Gordon Thurston spoke for thirty minutes, a moving and sometimes humorous account of a woman he had never met.

THE NEXT DAY we drove out to the cemetery to take pictures of the grave. The flowers were gone; there was not a trace of them, no petals scattered about, no arrangements tossed in garbage bins. They'd been stolen in the night. This is what we were told when we phoned the funeral home to complain. Who would steal funeral flowers? For what possible reason? It happens sometimes, they told us; unfortunately the cemetery isn't policed at night. The coffin was gone, too, though we were assured it was under the bare mound of dirt.

I thought of the two attendants. Maybe they were running a mom-and-pop operation boosting graveside flowers and selling them back to the florist, or to mourners looking for a bargain. It would be simple enough to replace the tags with blank ones, change the tribute ribbons from "Mother" to "Father." Who would know? Otherwise, what? Roving maniacs? Weirdos with funeral fetishes?

Still, those flowers being stolen made me mad. Those flowers were the least we could do.

FAMILY BAGGAGE

I. MAKEOVER

May Day weekend. Your older sister visits. And her husband who says, at sixty-four, he's through being an architect, it's a rat race—from now on he's taking acting lessons, he's going to be an actor. He shows us his promo picture, a large, smiling headshot he says he hates, but he also says, what the hell, it's got me a few commercial jobs. Your sister, your mother, and me are sitting outside in the sun and your sister's telling me about a new hair product from Clairol that hides the gray because, let's face it, she says, I've got enough gray to warrant a major operation. She says she'll personally escort me to Shoppers Drug Mart to pick out the colour that matches my own. Not only that, she'll supervise the makeover back home. Never one to refuse a gift, I agree, but nervously, thinking of last night when she gave me a lipstick, one she'd bought for herself but was the wrong shade for her skin. I wore it to dinner, for drinks and snacks at the only bar in the city that carried NTN, the National Trivia Network game, the game they said we'd love, they play it all the time at The Keg in Calgary. The new lipstick turned bright orange and I noticed two or three men (all right, they were old) looking at me in *that* way in the bar, but later in bed you said, I hate that lipstick, it makes you look like a cadaver, so maybe the older men were looking at me more in solidarity than in lust. But now as we're sitting together on the lawn your sister's husband joins us. He's got one of my books in his hand and he's just read the piece about Gertrude Stein and Alice Toklas and he says, I don't understand, you talk about Alice being the wife, was Stein a man? And I say, no, no they're famous lesbians but, of course, they couldn't be obvious in the 20s, 30s, and 40s. At which point your mother, hearing the word lesbian, perks up and says, That woman? I sat beside her on the plane from Toronto last year and I don't care what anybody says, she's a wreck, her hair and clothes are terrible; if there's anybody that needs a makeover it's Gertrude Stein. And we look at your mother for several long moments before your sister says kindly, Oh, yes? Then I remember it was Gloria Steinem your mother sat beside but the conversation's moved on to acting in the movies and my book has been tossed on the lawn. Because your sister's husband is lathering his bare legs with suntan oil and telling us anxiously, I've got to get a tan, the last thing I'm going to be is an old man with chicken legs, you see them all the time, scrawny white legs sticking out of horrible nylon shorts; no one's going to give you a part in a movie if you look like that.

2. BONDING

You said the best part of the Vancouver trip wasn't the reading I gave on the fourth floor of a condemned building, in a room that contained nothing but a dozen black chairs and a tabletop scattered with leaflets about the revolution. It wasn't the paid-for hotel room with the window fifty yards from the on-ramp to the Granville Street Bridge, or the dinner in the Japanese restaurant with the poet and her girlfriend and the girlfriend buying dinner. It wasn't even driving in the city traffic, and the way you suddenly became urban, honking the horn and yelling at pedestrians. And it wasn't leaving the kids and your mother at home with frozen pizza and lukewarm threats, or having a few extra bucks in your pocket to buy chocolate yoghurt on the ferry, beer and chicken wings in the hotel bar. No, what made the trip for you happened after the reading, walking into the first bar in Kitsilano and telling the waiter you were looking for a guy called Doug and the waiter saying, he's over there with the two girls. It was the way we walked up and tapped Doug on the shoulder and how he turned around laughing, delighted to see you. It was the way he said, Jesus Christ you asshole, just like it was twenty, twenty-five years ago when you had that apartment together on 4th Avenue and both of you bartended in Gastown. Forget drums and that wild man stuff, you once told me; male bonding is when you get pissed with a friend, have a few laughs, puke your guts out, shit your pants, then do it again the next night.

3. RACE CAR

Christmas. A small dinner downstairs with your mother.

Someone's given her a set of battery operated lights that she can wear to read in bed, a light strapped to either side of her head like headlights. After dinner you darken the room, put these lights on *your* head and pretend you're a race car, making race-car sounds with your voice: *Vroom Vroom.* You're so good at it that you look and sound exactly like a car. We laugh and laugh. Laugh till it hurts. The kids, they'd be five and eight, stand by your side staring. Your brother falls off his chair holding his sides. He hasn't dressed up for Christmas; he's wearing his old blue sweater, his cords with a tear at the knee. His own kids are with their mother, his ex-girlfriend, miles away. Stop it, you're killing me, he tells you. But you keep up the performance: *Vroom Vroom.* Around curves, bending your body right or left, accelerating, slowing down, spluttering then revving up, a kind of music, a free form jazz. You speed up hills, slow down in traffic, then roar towards the open road. Besides your headlights, there's only the Christmas candles burning, and the tiny white lights covering the dried branch your mother uses as a Christmas tree, the branch she painted white and brought with her when she moved from Toronto. Happy with the party, she opens another bottle of wine and, filling our half-empty glasses, says: This is like the time your father and some fellas were playing with Chatty Cathy in the backyard and they had the doll in the middle of a circle, a bunch of them drinking and betting on what the doll would say next, taking turns pulling the cord on her back. We laughed that time too, she said, and I remember that of all the things Chatty Cathy said, the line that came up the most was "I'm wet. Please change me."

4. PICTURE

You take my picture. A full roll of film is used, thirty-six exposures. Black and white pictures taken against a white paper backdrop you've attached to the kitchen wall because, you say, this is where the afternoon light is best. Headshots, body shots, shots taken from a ladder, shots taken while crouched on the floor. Your subject wearing black in some pictures, white in others. Hair hanging loose or tied back, wearing makeup, earrings, scarves, a turtleneck sweater, a baggy white shirt. And you serious with the light meter, intent, pausing only to drink the red wine you said would keep things relaxed. A Hungarian wine, St. Stephen's Crown, a bargain at nine ninety-five. There's music playing, *Slim Harpo Live,* then Clarence Gatemouth Brown. The kids off somewhere; it's a Sunday afternoon, a bright day, whitecaps in the bay. That's good, you say about a certain pose of my head, a shoulder angle, a look. Two glasses of wine and the roll's taken; right away you develop the film. Which one will we choose? A while later you show me the contact sheet and I scream. Because I don't recognize the woman in the pictures: the hair's too thin, the smiling mouth too wide, the face lined, unlovely. The camera never lies, you tell me, your face a study in grimness. You say it again. I'm sick of hearing this, it does lie; it lies all the time, or else you lie, I say. What I don't say is this injured thought comes from a radio program I've recently heard. An interview on CBC with a certain poet and the four poems he read: one about wisteria, one about a cougar in a tree, one about a spawning salmon, and one about his lover in her bath. There's something lovely about a woman in her bath, the poet says, and as we all know, my lover is very, very beautiful. I'm going to have a bath, I tell you, and what you say is: we can shoot another roll of film, maybe in the early evening, the light is kinder then. And I say, sure, why not? Give me kindness. But some time later, after the heat of the bath water has subsided, you're kneeling at the side of the tub and lathering soap on your hands. Slowly, intently, you're washing my legs, arms, back, and breasts. Then rinsing my body with the bath water you've cupped in your hands.

ACKNOWLEDGEMENTS

Earlier, and, in some cases, different versions of the stories in this book have been published as follows: "The Secret Lives of Litterbugs" in *Imagining British Columbia—Land, Memory & Place*, Daniel Francis, Editor, Anvil Press, 2008; "Baked Salmon" in *Apples Under the Bed—Recollections and Recipes from B.C. Writers and Artists*, Joan Coldwell, Editor, Hedgerow Press, 2007; "Skidney" in *Girls Around the House*, Polestar Press, 1999; "Condom Run" in *Girls Around the House*, Polestar Press, 1999; "Ritardando" in *Girls Around the House*, Polestar Press, 1999; "Family Baggage" in *Geist* Magazine, 1999; "The Princess, the Queen & the Withered King" in *What's True, Darling*, Polestar Press, 1997; "Tic Tac Doe" in *What's True, Darling*, Polestar Press, 1997; "The Panelist" as "Panelist School" in *Girls Around the House*, Polestar Press, 1999; "The Judge," as "You Be the Judge," in the *Vancouver Sun*, Nov 20, 2004, Rebecca Wigod, Editor; "Notes on the Wedding" in *Geist* Magazine,

Issue #71, January, 2009, Mary Schendlinger, Editor.

The stories contained herein are as true and as accurate as memory allows; some names have been changed for privacy's sake.

With love and thanks for permissions given: Shirley Taillefer, Doreen Jones, Bob Jones, Terry Farrant, Bill Farrant, and Anna Farrant. Many thanks also to Carolyn Swayze and Jane Warren for their enthusiasm for this project, to Pauline Holdstock for countless years of camaraderie, and to Vicky Husband for all manner of support and friendship.

In remembrance of Ernie Sexton (1906-1970), W.D. (Billy) Gibson (1906-1981), Elsie Sexton (1905-2003), and Sara (Nana) Farrant (1912-2005).

Support from the Seaview Cultural Fund is gratefully acknowledged.